Houghton Mifflin

English

Shirley Haley-James   John Warren Stewig

Marcus T. Ballenger   Jacqueline L. Chaparro   Nancy C. Millett

June Grant Shane   C. Ann Terry

HOUGHTON   MIFFLIN   COMPANY   BOSTON

Atlanta   Dallas   Geneva, Illinois   Palo Alto   Princeton   Toronto

Acknowledgments

The publisher has made every effort to locate each owner of the copyrighted material reprinted here. Any information enabling the publisher to rectify or credit any reference is welcome.

A Chair for My Mother by Vera B. Williams. Copyright © 1982 by Vera B. Williams. By permission of Greenwillow Books (A Division of William Morrow & Company), and published in Great Britain by Julia MacRae Books, London.

"Clouds," from *The Cloud Book* by Tomie de Paola. Copyright © 1975 by Tomie de Paola. Reprinted by permission of Holiday House.

"The Day We Saw the Sun Come Up," from *The Day We Saw The Sun Come Up* by Alice E. Goudey. Text copyright © 1961 by Alice Goudey. Reprinted with the permission of the author.

"Dear Daddy" from *Dear Daddy* by Philippe Dupasquier. Copyright © 1985 by Philippe Dupasquier. Adapted with permission of Bradbury Press, an Affiliate of Macmillan, Inc., and Anderson Press Limited.

"Gloria Who Might Be My Best Friend" in *The Stories Julian Tells* by Ann Cameron. Copyright © 1981 by Ann Cameron. Reprinted by permission of Pantheon Books, a division of Random House, Inc. and Curtis Brown, Ltd.

"I Speak" by Arnold L. Shapiro excerpted from *Poems And Rhymes*, Volume 1 of CHILDCRAFT—THE HOW AND WHY LIBRARY. © 1982 World Book, Inc.

"More Potatoes," from *More Potatoes!* by Millicent Selsam. Pictures by Ben Shecter. Text copyright © 1972 by Millicent Selsam. Pictures copyright © 1972 by Ben Shecter. Reprinted by permission of Harper & Row, Publishers, Inc., Millicent Selsam, and Ben Shecter.

Nobody by Patience Brewster. Copyright © 1982 by Patience Brewster. Reprinted by permission of Clarion Books/Ticknor & Fields, a Houghton Mifflin Company.

1995 Impression
Copyright © 1990 by Houghton Mifflin Company. All rights reserved.

No part of this work may be reproduced or transmitted in any form or by any means, electronic or mechanical, including photocopying and recording, or by any information storage or retrieval system without the prior written permission of Houghton Mifflin Company unless such copying is expressly permitted by federal copyright law. Address inquiries to School Permissions, Houghton Mifflin Company, 222 Berkeley Street, Boston, MA 02116.

Printed in U.S.A.
ISBN: 0–395–50262–4

IJ-DP-9654

Nothing Sticks Like a Shadow by Ann Tompert, illustrated by Lynn Munsinger. Illustrations copyright © 1984 by Lynn Munsinger. Reprinted by permission of Houghton Mifflin Company.

Brief Quotations

from *Writing* by Murray McCain. Copyright © 1964 Murray McCain. Reprinted by permission of Farrar, Straus & Giroux, Inc. and Russell & Volkening Inc.   (p. 1)

from "The Little Turtle" in *Collected Poems* by Vachel Lindsay. Copyright 1920 by Macmillan Publishing Company, renewed 1948 by Elizabeth C. Lindsay. Reprinted with permission of Macmillan Publishing Company.   (p. 36)

from "Blum" by Dorothy Aldis, reprinted by permission of G. P. Putnam's Sons from *Here, There and Everywhere* by Dorothy Aldis, copyright 1927, 1928, copyright renewed © 1955, 1956 by Dorothy Aldis.   (p. 94)

from *Along Sandy Trails* by Ann Nolan Clark. Text copyright © 1969 by Ann Nolan Clark. Reprinted by permission of Viking Penguin, Inc.   (p. 124)

from "Curb Your Cloud" by Richard García. Copyright © 1979 by Richard García. Reprinted with permission of the author.   (p. 124)

from "Tiptoe" in *Dogs & Dragons, Trees & Dreams: A Collection of Poems* by Karla Kuskin. Copyright © 1958 by Karla Kuskin. Reprinted by permission of Harper & Row, Publishers, Inc.   (p. 150)

from "How to Eat a Poem" in *JAMBOREE Rhymes for All Times* by Eve Merriam. Copyright © 1962, 1964, 1966, 1973, 1984 by Eve Merriam. All rights reserved. Reprinted by permission of Marian Reiner for the author.   (p. 188)

from "Spinning Song" in *Today Is Saturday* by Zilpha Keatley Snyder. Copyright © 1969 by Zilpha Keatley Snyder. Reprinted with the permission of the author.   (p. 236)

from "No One Writes a Letter to a Snail" by Maxine Kumin. Text © 1962 by Maxine Kumin. Reprinted by permission of Curtis Brown, Ltd.   (p. 296)

Entries from *Houghton Mifflin Primary Dictionary*, by *American Heritage Dictionary*. Copyright © 1980, renewed 1986 by Houghton Mifflin Company. Reprinted by permission of Houghton Mifflin Company.

Grateful acknowledgment is given to Anne Greenwood for permission to adapt and reprint original material as student writing models in The Writing Process lessons.

(Acknowledgments continued on page 368.)

Table of Contents

4

Literature and Writing: Letters

Writing has many uses.
Think what would happen
If everyone talked at once.

Murray McCain
from **Writing**

How do potatoes get from the ground
to the store?

More Potatoes

By Millicent Selsam

One day at school, Sue asked her teacher,
"Can the class go to see a warehouse?"

"What warehouse?" asked the teacher.

"Well," said Sue, "my mother needed
potatoes. I went to the store to get them. The
storekeeper gave me his last two pounds. I
asked him where he was going to get more
potatoes. He said that a truck brings the
potatoes from a warehouse."

The teacher said to the class, "How many of
you want to visit this warehouse?"

They all raised their hands.

The next Monday, the class rode to the
warehouse. Mr. Green showed them the trucks
being loaded with potatoes and other
vegetables.

"But where do the potatoes come from?" asked Sue.

"From farms," said Mr. Green.

"May I take these children to a potato farm?" asked the teacher.

"Well," said Mr. Green. "You can try Mr. Bartilucci's farm. It is not too far from the city."

One Tuesday, the class rode out to the farm. Mr. Bartilucci was waiting for them.

"The potato plants are already growing," said Mr. Bartilucci. "I planted them in May."

"Do you plant them from seeds?" asked the teacher.

"No," said Mr. Bartilucci. "We plant small potatoes. We call them seed potatoes." He took a potato from his pocket and cut it in four pieces.

"These are the pieces of potato we plant. Each piece must have at least one or two eyes. The eyes are the places on the potato where the buds are. New potato plants grow from these buds."

"How do you plant them?" asked one of the boys. "Do you go along and drop them in the ground?"

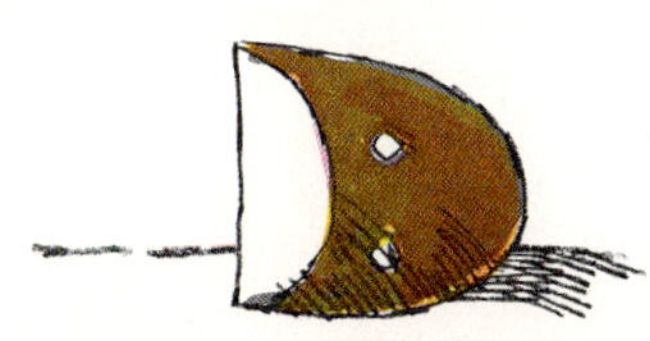

"Oh, no," said Mr. Bartilucci. "The farm is too big for that. I have a machine that plants the potatoes."

He took the class to the barn to show them the machine. Then the class followed Mr. Bartilucci to the field. As far as they could see, there were rows of green plants.

"But where are the potatoes?" asked Sue.

Mr. Bartilucci took a shovel and dug under one plant. Then he lifted the whole plant out of the earth. The potatoes were small, but they were there. They were on the part of the plant that had been growing under the ground.

"They will grow bigger all through the summer," said Mr. Bartilucci.

"Who digs up the potatoes when they are ready?" asked Sue.

"A big machine digs them up in September," said Mr. Bartilucci. "We wash the potatoes and put them in bags. Then our trucks take the bags to the warehouse."

"And then the warehouse trucks take the potatoes to the stores," said Sue. "Now we know where potatoes come from!"

Think and Discuss

1. Where are potatoes planted? How do potatoes get from the ground to the store?

2. Why do you think the farmer used a machine to dig up his potatoes?

3. An **author** is someone who writes a story. Who is the author of "More Potatoes"? Why do you think she wrote this story?

13

STEP 1: PREWRITING

How to Choose a Topic

Mr. Scott's class wanted to write a class story. They talked about some special things they had done. Mr. Scott listed their ideas.

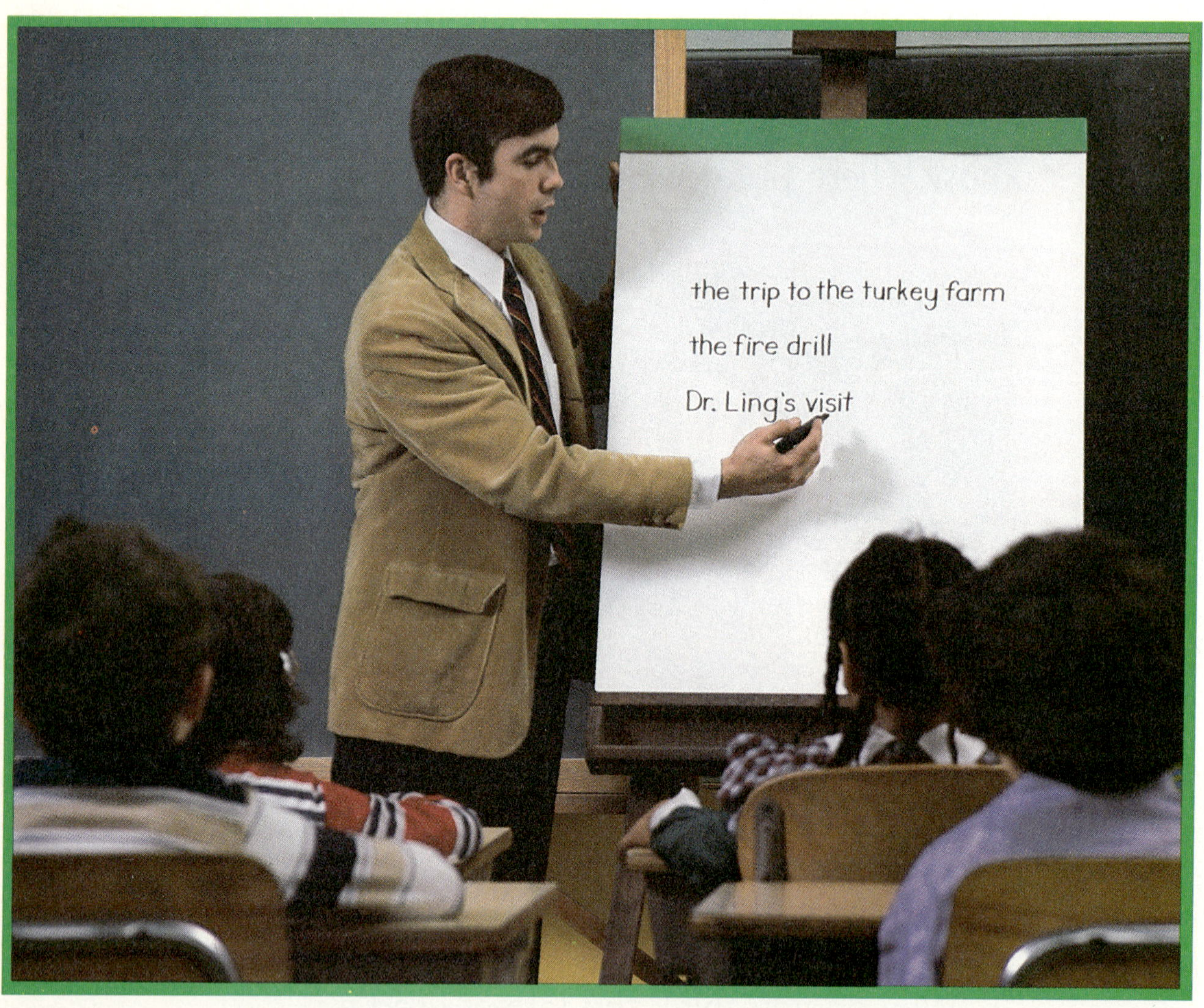

The class thought about each idea. The trip had been fun, but not everyone had gone. The fire drill idea was boring. Dr. Ling's visit had also been fun. Everyone had been in school that day. They decided to write about that.

One of the students in Mr. Scott's class circled their idea for a class story.

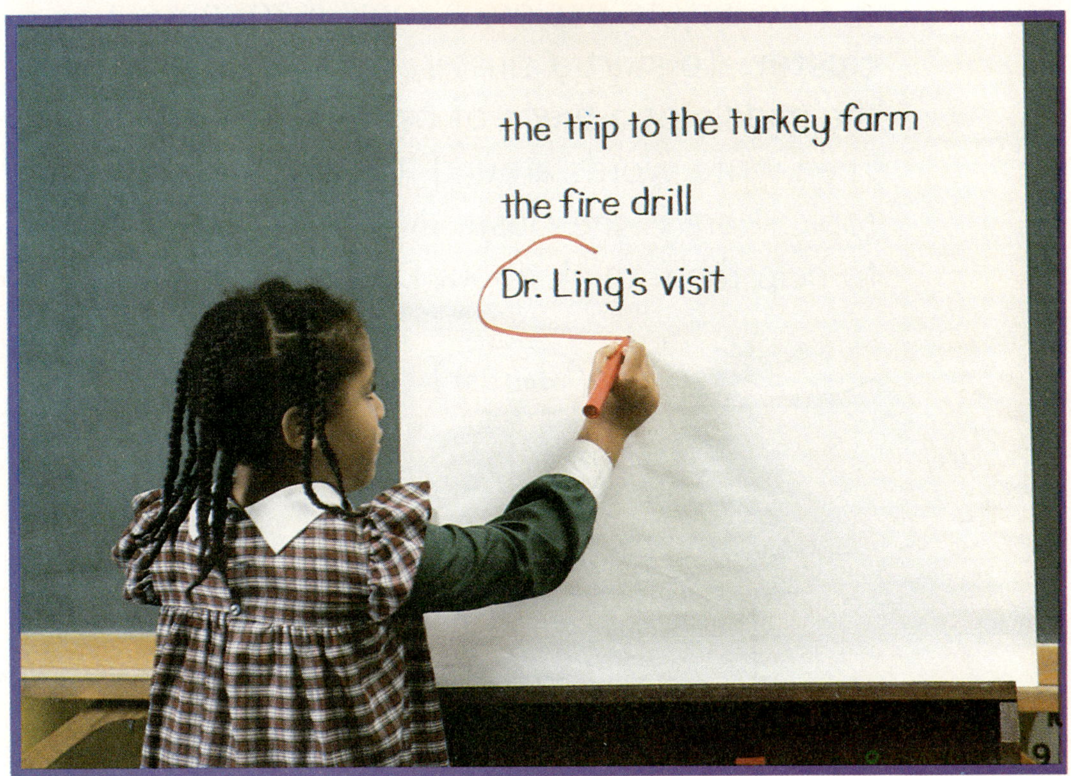

Choosing Your Topic

1. **Think and discuss** Think about special times your class has had. Use the ideas above to help you. Help your teacher list your ideas.

2. **Choose** Answer these questions about each idea.

   Would we like to write about this?
   Do we remember enough about it?
   Will a reader be interested?

   Choose an idea. Have someone circle it.

3. **Try it** What will you write? Do the activity under "How to Explore Your Topic" on the next page.

Getting Ready to Write **15**

How to Explore Your Topic

One way to explore a topic is to make a **cluster.** To start a cluster, write your topic in the middle of a piece of paper. Circle the topic. Then write words around it that tell about your topic. Here is the cluster Mr. Scott's class made to help them think about Dr. Ling's visit.

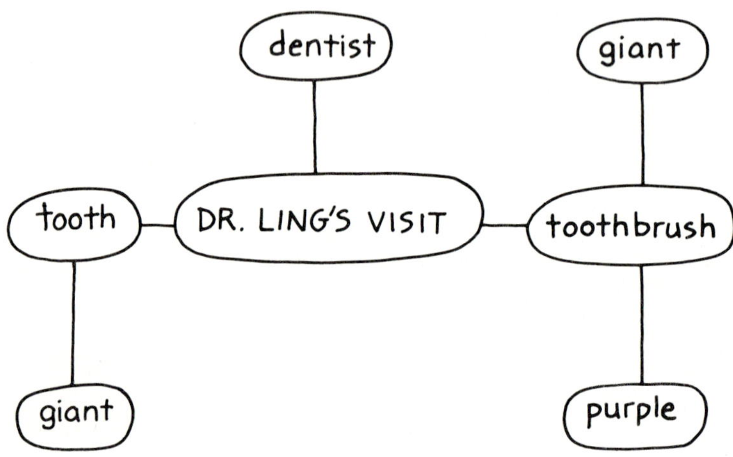

Exploring Your Topic

Make a cluster with your class. Write and circle one of the words below. What other words does it make you think of? Write them around the first word. Draw lines to join your words. Draw your cluster in the box.

singing   recess   Saturdays   lunch

How to Write a First Draft

The children were ready to write their first draft. A **first draft** is a first try.

Mr. Scott wrote the first draft on the chart. The class told him what to write. They would make changes later.

> A dentist visited our class.
>
> Her name was Dr. Ling. She
>
> came with a tooth and a
>
> toothbrush. ~~We saw~~ They were
>
> so big! They made us laugh.
>
> A writer also came one day.

Think and Discuss
- What is the story about?
- Which sentence does not tell about the dentist's visit?
- What else would you like to know?
- Why are some words crossed out?

Writing Your First Draft

1. **Talk about it** Talk together about what you want to say. Answer these questions.

   What important things can we tell?
   How can we make the story interesting?

2. **Tell and write** Tell your story to your teacher. Your teacher will write the first draft. You can make changes later.

How to Revise

The children read their first draft aloud. They talked about ways to make their story better.

Reading and responding

Then they revised their class story. Look at the revised story on the next page.

A dentist visited our class.

Her name was Dr. Ling. She came with a *giant* tooth and a *giant purple* toothbrush. ~~We saw~~ They were so big! They made us laugh. *We used them to learn the best* ~~A writer also came one day.~~ *way to brush our teeth.*

Think and Discuss

- Which sentence was crossed out? Why?
- Which words were added? Why?
- Which sentence was added? Why?

Revising on Your Own

1. **Read aloud** Listen as someone reads your class story. Think about these questions.

   What else would a reader like to know? Does each sentence tell about the story?

2. **Revise** Talk about ways to make the story better. Help your teacher make changes.

See the Thesaurus on page 347.

How to Proofread

Everyone in Mr. Scott's class copied the story. Then they proofread their papers. When they proofread, they looked for mistakes. They used proofreading marks to correct their mistakes.

Here is Andrea's proofread story.

Andrea's story after proofreading

> A dentist visited our class. Her name was Dr. Ling. She came with a giant tooth and a giant purple toothbrush. they were so big! They made us laugh. We used them to learn the best way to brush our teeth.

Think and Discuss
- Why did Andrea add a capital letter?
- What end mark did she add? Why?
- What spelling did she correct?

Proofreading on Your Own

1. Proofreading Practice There are two mistakes in each sentence. Write the sentences correctly.

a. where did Sam go.

b. he wint to the park.

c. what did he find

2. Copy and proofread Copy your class story. Then proofread your class story. Use the checklist and proofreading marks to help you.

<table>
<tr><td>

Proofreading Checklist

☑ **1.** Did I begin each sentence with a capital letter?
☑ **2.** Did I use correct end marks?
☑ **3.** Did I spell each word correctly?

</td><td>

Proofreading Marks

∧ Add
— Take out
≡ Make a capital letter
/ Make a small letter

</td></tr>
</table>

How to Publish

The children in Mr. Scott's class were proud of their story. They thought of different ways to show their story.

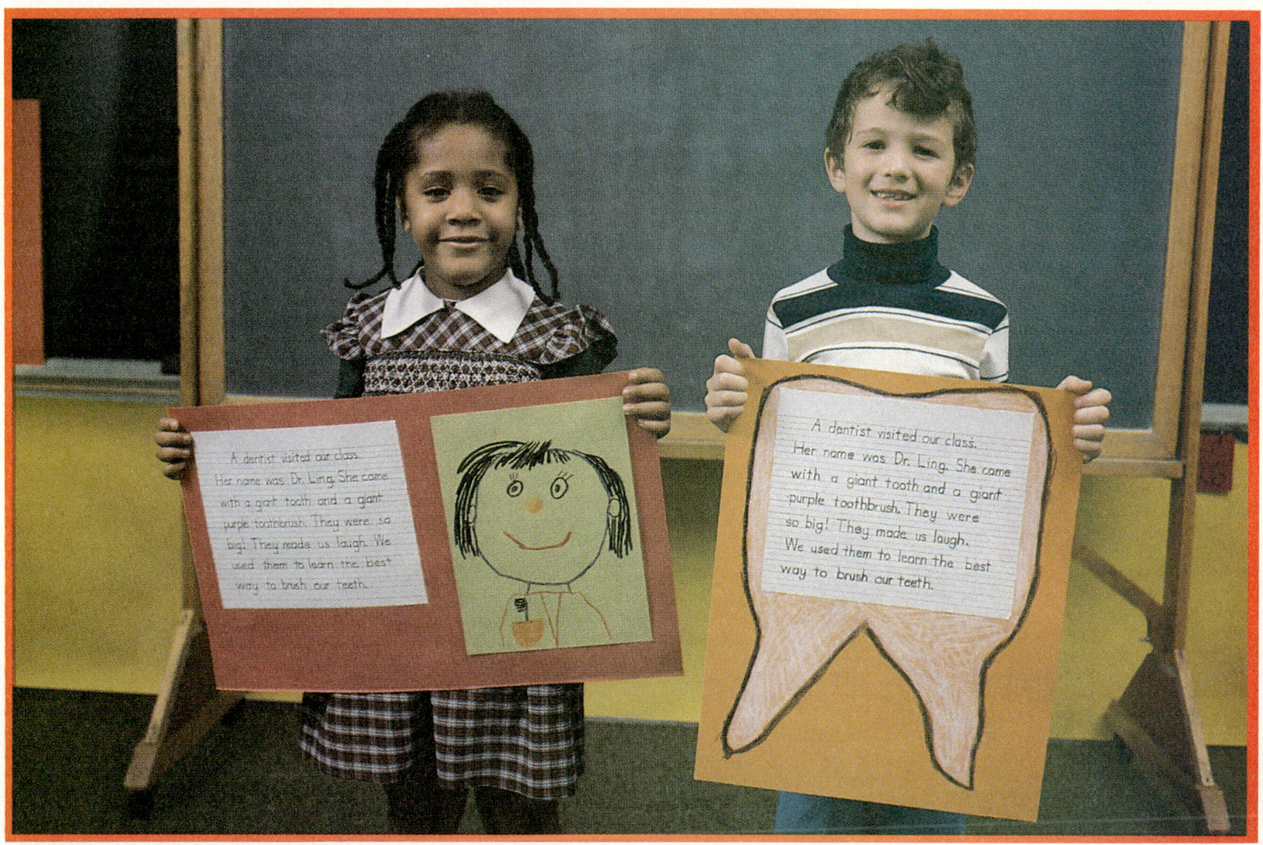

Publishing on Your Own

Share Think of a special way to show your story. Share it with your class or with someone at home.

Ideas for Sharing

- Make a storybook. Draw a picture to go with your story. Make a book cover. Read and show your storybook.
- Display your story on the bulletin board.

Getting Ready
Listening and Speaking

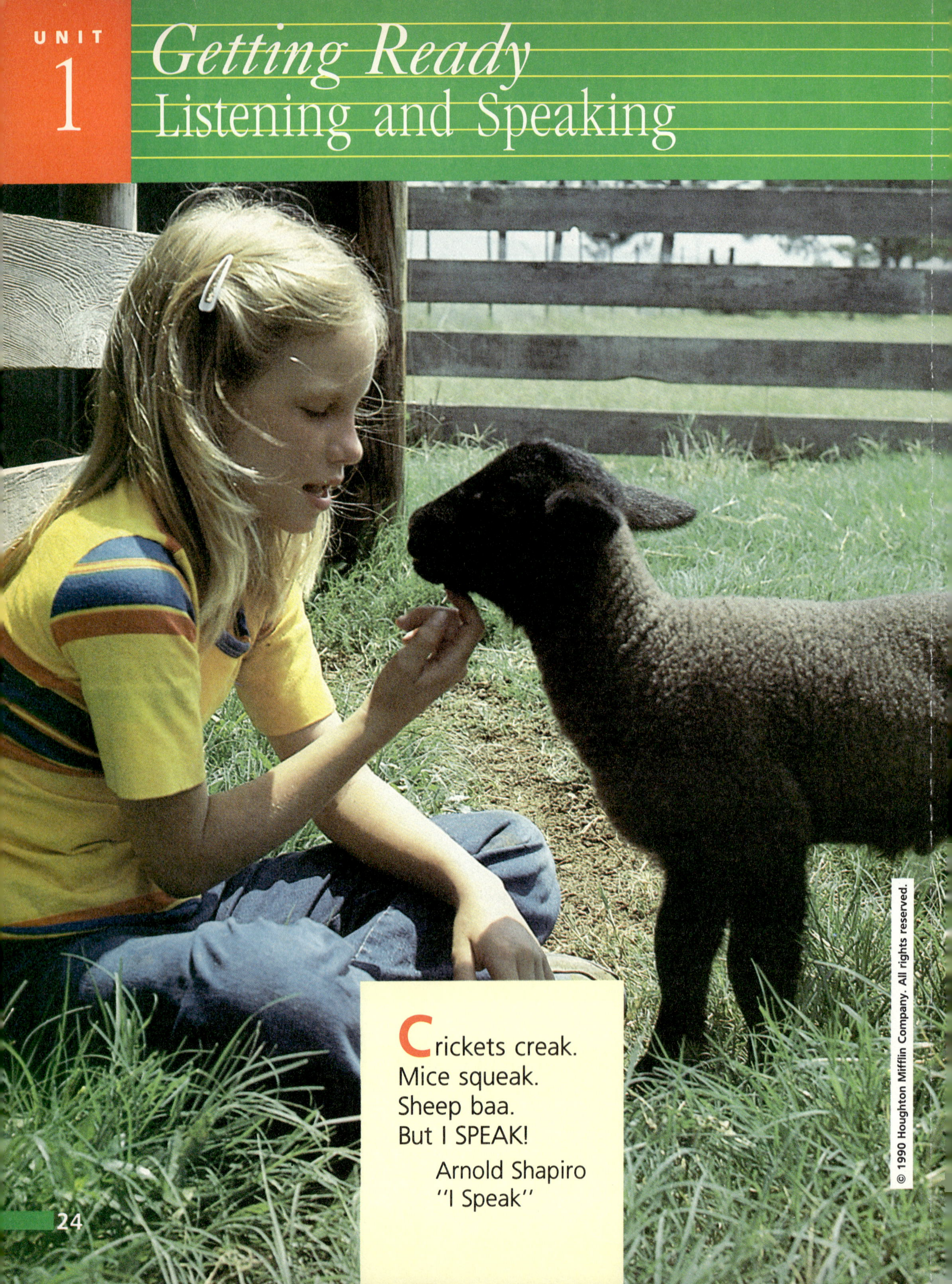

1 | Being a Good Listener and Speaker

Are you a good listener? Look at the picture. Listen as your teacher reads to you.

Point to the thing your teacher read about. Are you a good speaker? Look at the picture again. Tell about something you see.

Listening and Speaking Helps

1. Listen carefully.
2. Ask questions if you do not understand.
3. Think about what you will say.
4. Speak loudly and clearly.
5. Take turns.

Practice Listen as your teacher reads to you. Tell something about Ricky.

Read this discussion. Who did not talk about the class picnic?

Discussion Helps

1. Be a good listener. Do not talk when someone else is talking.
2. Speak so that everyone can hear you.
3. Keep to the topic.

Practice Susan wrote about her trip to a farm. Read this class discussion about her story. Cross out the sentence that does not keep to the topic.

Gina: When did you go to the farm?

Sam: What animals did you see besides pigs?

Ben: I went on a boat ride once.

3 | Listening for Information

Listen carefully when someone gives you facts, or information, about something. Listen for details that answer the questions <u>Who?</u> <u>What?</u> <u>Where?</u> <u>When?</u> or <u>How?</u>

Listen as your teacher reads some information about plastics. Can you answer these questions?

1. What are the colors and shapes of plastics?
2. What are plastics used for?

When you listen carefully, you can learn many new things. Use this help when you listen for information.

Listening Help

Listen for facts that answer the questions <u>Who?</u> <u>What?</u> <u>Where?</u> <u>When?</u> or <u>How?</u>

Practice Listen as your teacher reads to you. Listen for answers to these questions.

1. What is coming?
2. Where will it be held?
3. When is it?
4. Who is taking the book orders?

Read what Carol and Bob said on the telephone. What message did Carol take?

Carol: Hello.
  Bob: Hello. May I speak to your brother, please?
Carol: He isn't here. May I take a message?
  Bob: This is Bob. Ask your brother to call me, please. My number is 892-1460.
Carol: I'll tell him to call Bob at 892-1460.
  Bob: Yes. Thank you. Good-by.
Carol: Good-by.

Telephone Helps

1. Write the caller's name.
2. Write the caller's telephone number.
3. Check to make sure the name and number are correct.

Practice Listen as your teacher reads another call.

1. Who called? ________________

2. What is the message? ________________

3. What is the caller's telephone number? ________________

5 | Calling for Help

How would you call for help?

When you use the telephone to call for help, do these things.

Telephone Helps

1. Find the right number. Call the operator if you cannot find the number.
2. Dial the number or operator.
3. When someone answers, remember to do these things.

   - Tell your name.
   - Tell the address where help is needed.
   - Tell what happened.

Practice Write these telephone numbers and your address.

1. Operator ________________________________

2. My telephone number ________________________

3. My address ________________________________

The **topic** of a story is the one thing a story is about. The **main idea** of a story is a sentence that tells the most about the topic.

Listen as your teacher reads to you. Which word below names the topic?

ball   penny   circles

Which sentence below tells the main idea?

1. A plate is a circle.
2. Each day we use many circles.

Listening Helps

1. Listen for the one thing a story is about. That is the **topic.**
2. Listen for the sentence that tells the most about the topic. That is the **main idea.**

Practice Listen for the topic. Then write the sentence that tells the main idea.

Cars have many tires.
Cars have many differences.
Cars may be painted pink.

7 | Listening to Tell What Will Happen

Often when you listen to a story, you can tell what will happen before it really happens. Certain words will help you figure it out. Listen as your teacher reads you part of a story. Will Rachael get to play in the first soccer game?

Use these helps when listening to tell what will happen.

Listening Helps

1. Listen for words or sentences that give you clues.
2. Use things you already know.
3. Use the clues and the things you know to figure out what will happen.

Practice Listen as your teacher reads to you. Listen for what will happen.

Reading a Play

A **play** is a story that is meant to be acted out or read aloud. Reading a play aloud can be fun. Remember to use these helps.

Speaking Helps

1. First, read the play to yourself.
2. Read the character's words as you think the character might say them.
3. Practice until you can read your part smoothly.
4. Read loudly and clearly.

Practice Read the play to yourself. Then with your class, choose parts and read the play aloud.

The Mice Have a Meeting

**from the story by Aesop
retold by Marie Gaudette**

CHARACTERS:
Storyteller
Oldest Mouse
Older Mouse
Old Mouse
Young Mouse
Younger Mouse
Youngest Mouse

SETTING:
The setting is the mice's living room. It is inside a wall of an old house. At one end is a mouse-hole door.

TIME:
The time is early one night.

Storyteller:	Once upon a time, six mice lived in a big old house. They had only one problem. A large cat lived there too. The mice had to be very careful.
Older Mouse:	That was close, Old Mouse! I am tired of hiding from the cat!
Old Mouse:	The cat is always chasing us. What can we do, Older Mouse?
Older Mouse:	It is time for the weekly mouse meeting. Someone will think of a plan.
Storyteller:	Oldest Mouse came in and sat down. The other mice walked in, one by one. Then Oldest Mouse stood up slowly.
Oldest Mouse:	Let the weekly mouse meeting come to order! What do we need to talk about tonight?

Old Mouse: Please, Oldest Mouse, let's talk about the cat. We are tired of this danger! The cat moves very quietly. How can we warn each other when the cat is near?

Storyteller: All the mice talked at once. But no one had a plan. Then Oldest Mouse raised a paw. The other mice stopped talking.

Oldest Mouse: I know what must be done. We must find a small bell. The bell must be tied to the ribbon on the cat's neck. Then it will not matter how quietly the cat moves. We will hear the bell and be warned!

Young Mouse: What a good idea!

Younger Mouse: Our troubles are over! Oldest Mouse is so wise!

 Reading a Play

Storyteller:	All the mice clapped their paws. Only Youngest Mouse did not clap. He looked very unhappy. Then he held up his paw.
Youngest Mouse:	Please, may I speak?
Old Mouse:	What is there to say? The plan is perfect!
Youngest Mouse:	Please, Oldest Mouse, may I speak?
Oldest Mouse:	Hush! Let Youngest Mouse speak.
Youngest Mouse:	Please, Oldest Mouse, I have just one question. Who will put the bell on the cat?
Storyteller:	Youngest Mouse sat down very quietly. And no one said anything at all.

Language and Usage
The Sentence

1 | What Is a Sentence?

A **sentence** tells what someone or something did.

> The boy played.
> The toy train went fast.

Who played? What did the boy do?
What went fast? What did the toy train do?

Guided Practice Match the groups of words to make sentences. Say the sentences.

★ The girl   stopped.

1. The train   popped.

2. The doll   laughed.

3. The balloon   smiled.

Now write the sentences.

1. ________________________________

2. ________________________________

3. ________________________________

Summing up

▶ A **sentence** tells what someone or something did.

★ The bell   kicks.

1. The sun   toots.

2. The baby   rings.

3. The horn   melts.

4. The plane   shines.

5. The snow   flies.

Now write the sentences.

★ The bell rings.

1.

2.

3.

4.

5.

Writing Application: Something I Do
Write about something you do. Use sentences.

For Extra Practice, see p. 57.

2 | Naming Part

Jason went to the circus.

A **monkey** walked on a rope.

Who went to the circus? What walked on a rope? The **naming part** of a sentence tells who or what.

Guided Practice Look at the picture. Say a naming part from the Word Box to begin each sentence about the picture.

| A dog |
| A bear |
| A girl |
| A clown |

★  <u>A bear</u> sat on a ball.

1. _____ had a red nose.

2. _____ stood on a horse.

3. _____ jumped.

Now write the sentences.

1. ___________________________________

2. ___________________________________

3. ___________________________________

Summing up

▶ The **naming part** of a sentence tells whom or what a sentence is about.

Independent Practice

A. Write the naming part from the Word Box
that fits each sentence.

Birds	Cats
Rabbits	Dogs

★ ________ Cats ________ purr.

2. ________________ hop.

1. ________________ fly.

3. ________________ bark.

B. Write the naming part from the Word Box
that fits each sentence.

The water	The ball
The chick	The boy

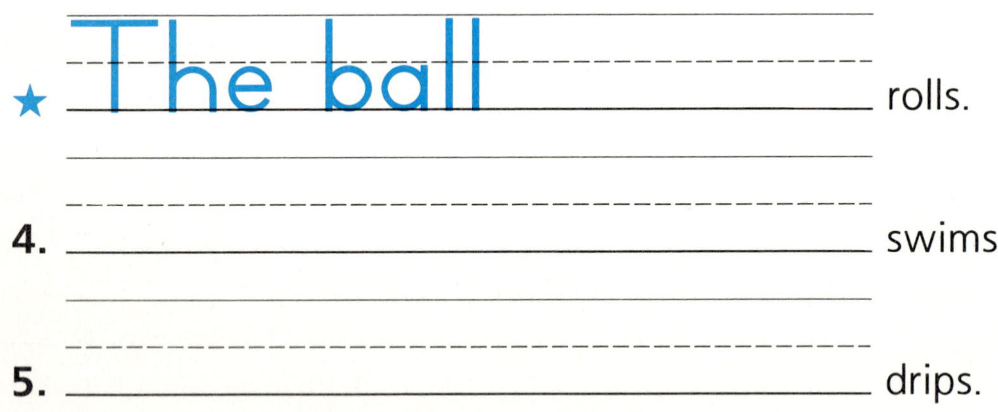

★ ________ The ball ________ rolls.

4. ________________ swims.

5. ________________ drips.

6. ________________ peeps.

Writing Application: A Toy I Like
Write about a toy you like. Use sentences.

For Extra Practice, see p. 58.

3 | Action Part

The **action part** of a sentence tells what is happening. What is Ken doing?

Ken follows the signs.   Ken slides.

Guided Practice Look at the picture. Say an action part from the Word Box to finish each sentence.

slides down a pole	jumps over a pool
show what to do	watches

★ A chipmunk <u>watches</u>.

1. Annie ____.
2. Ken ____.
3. The signs ____.

Now write the sentences.

1. _______________________

2. _______________________

3. _______________________

Summing up

▶ The **action part** tells what is happening.

Independent Practice

A. Finish each sentence. Write an action part
from the Word Box.

writes books	grows food
makes bread	makes us well

★ A baker  makes bread __________.

1. A doctor __________.

2. A writer __________.

3. A farmer __________.

B. Write an action part for each sentence.

★ Mother works in a bank __________.

4. A friend __________.

5. A teacher __________.

Writing Application: **What I Like to Do**
Write about something you like to do. Use
sentences.

For Extra Practice, see p. 59.

4 | Is It a Sentence?

Every sentence must have a naming part and an action part. Read these sentences.

Ben watches the frog.
Ben watches the frog.

Tell the naming part. Tell the action part.
These groups of words are not sentences.
Which group of words needs a naming part?
Which group needs an action part?

swims fast   an ant

Guided Practice Tell which groups of words are sentences. Then write the sentences.

★ The wind blew.   sentence

1. The fish swam.   **3.** Birds sang.
2. green legs   **4.** A frog jumped.

Summing up

▶ A sentence has a naming part and an action part.

Independent Practice

A. Write **yes** before each sentence. Write **no** before each group of words that is not a sentence.

yes ★ Plants grow.

_____ **1.** floats away

_____ **2.** deep water

_____ **3.** A stick snaps.

B. Find the sentences below. Draw a line under each sentence. Then write the sentences.

★ <u>Tom sat on a rock.</u>   A snake took a nap.

a pretty lake   spun a web

Tony fed the ducks.   Bees buzzed.

★ _Tom sat on a rock._

4. _____________________________

5. _____________________________

6. _____________________________

Writing Application: Description
Write about a pond. Use sentences.

5 | Telling Sentences

A **telling sentence** tells something. It begins with a capital letter. It ends with a period.

> **S**ome animals live on farms.
> **H**orses live there.

Guided Practice Tell how to make each telling sentence correct.

★ chickens lay eggs
Chickens lay eggs.

1. the sheep are in a pen.
2. Pigs roll in the mud
3. cows eat grass

Now write the sentences correctly.

1. _______________________________

2. _______________________________

3. _______________________________

Summing up

> ▶ A **telling sentence** tells something. It begins with a capital letter. It ends with a period.

Independent Practice

A. Draw a line under each correct telling sentence.

★ <u>The wind blows.</u>

the wind blows.

1. It is hot

It is hot.

2. The dogs sleep.

the dogs sleep.

3. The cat naps

The cat naps.

4. The girl yawns.

the girl yawns

B. Write these telling sentences correctly.

★ that house is on fire

That house is on fire.

5. Someone called the firehouse

6. the fire truck is here

7. The fire is out

Writing Application: An Experience
Write about your day with an animal.

For Extra Practice, see p. 61.

6 | Questions

A **question** asks something. It begins with a capital letter. It ends with a question mark.

Does the squirrel see the nut**?**
Will the squirrel eat it**?**

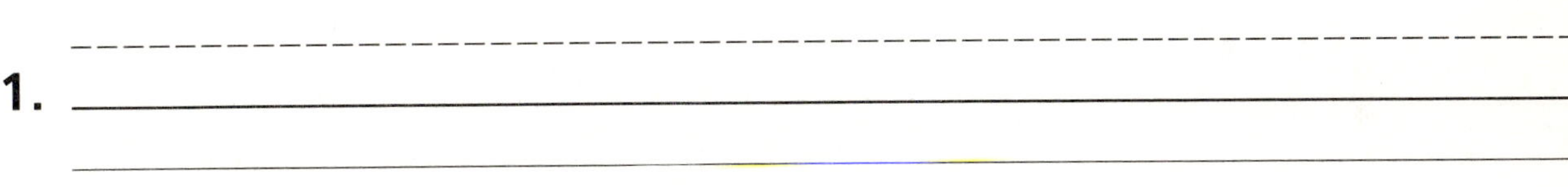

Guided Practice Tell how to make each question correct.

★ what does it eat   What does it eat?

1. will it eat seeds?
2. is the squirrel red
3. where does it live

Now write the questions correctly.

1. _______________________________________

2. _______________________________________

3. _______________________________________

Summing up

▶ A **question** asks something. It begins with a capital letter. It ends with a question mark.

Independent Practice

A. Draw a line under each correct question.

  ★ Do you see stars

  <u>Do you see stars?</u>

1. is the moon out?

  Is the moon out?

2. Is that a rocket?

  Is that a rocket

3. will it go far

  Will it go far?

4. Where is it going?

  where is it going?

B. Write these questions correctly.

  ★ have you seen a rocket

Have you seen a rocket?

5. Was it very big

6. did it fly away?

7. where did it go

Writing Application: Questions
Write some questions about flying in a rocket.

For Extra Practice, see p. 62.

7 | Which Kind of Sentence?

You have learned that a telling sentence ends with a period. You have also learned that a question ends with a question mark.

Guided Practice Tell if a sentence is a telling sentence or a question.

★ Where is the store   question

1. Will we go to the store
2. I am going now

Now write the sentences correctly.

1. ____

2. ____

Summing up

▶ A sentence tells something or asks a question. A telling sentence ends with a period. A question ends with a question mark.

A. Write **T** before each telling sentence.
Write **Q** before each question.

T ★ A bee is a bug.   _____ **2.** Bees make honey.

_____ **1.** Do bees like flowers?   _____ **3.** How is honey made?

B. Write the sentences. Use capital letters and
end marks correctly.

★ is that rose red

Is that rose red?

4. the flower smells sweet

5. is the flower big

6. what color is the flower

Writing Application: **Descriptions**
Write about some shapes of flowers. Write
some questions about bees.

50   **Which Kind of Sentence?**   **For Extra Practice, see p. 63.**

Grammar-Writing Connection

Writing Clearly with Sentences

Read these groups of words.

The little boy
Rode his bike

The first word group tells who. The second group tells what is happening. If we put the two groups together, we will have one sentence that makes sense.

The little boy rode his bike.

Good writers use sentences that tell whom or what the sentence is about and what is happening. Good sentences make sense.

Revising Sentences

Complete each sentence.

★ The little black cat *purred* __________.

1. The circus clown __________.

2. __________ walked a tightrope.

3. __________ rode a spotted pony.

Grammar-Writing Connection

Doctor and Doll
by Norman Rockwell

Norman Rockwell painted pictures of life in America. This doctor has <u>two</u> visitors.

• What interesting things do you see?

Activities

1. **Write the doctor's report.** Is the doll sick or well? Write what the doctor says.
2. **Write a story.** Who is the girl? Why is she there? Write a story about her.

Check-up: Unit 2

What Is a Sentence? (page 37)

Draw lines to make sentences.

1. The plane   had a good time.

2. The ride   was bumpy.

3. The food   took off.

4. All of us   tasted good.

Naming Part and Action Part (pages 39, 41)

Choose a naming part or an action part from the Word Box to fit each sentence. Write the sentences.

The plane	was setting
talked to us	City lights
got off the plane	

5. The sun _______________.

6. ______________ were below us.

7. The pilot _______________.

8. ______________ landed.

9. We _______________.

Is It a Sentence? (page 43)

Write **yes** before the sentence. Write **no** before the words that are not a sentence.

_________ **10.** bright lights   _________ **11.** The city was hot.

Telling Sentences and Questions (pages 45, 47)

Write each sentence correctly. Begin each sentence with a capital letter. Use correct end marks.

12. that man sells balloons

13. did he let them go

14. green balloons float away

Which Kind of Sentence? (page 49)

Write **T** before each telling sentence. Write **Q** before each question.

_____ **15.** I like the park.   _____ **17.** Is it fun?

_____ **16.** Will you come?   _____ **18.** Children ride bikes.

Enrichment

Using Sentences

Zoo Interview

Pretend that you can
talk with a zoo animal.
Write three questions
to ask this animal on a sheet of paper. Skip
three lines below each question. Write the
animal's answers.

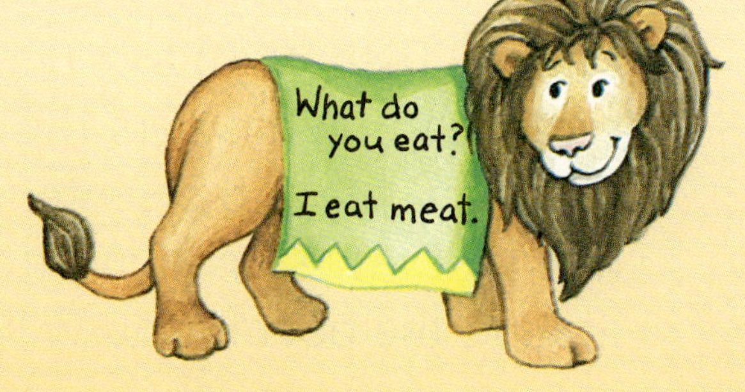

EXTRA! Draw and cut out a large picture of the
animal. Paste the questions and answers on it.

Silly Animals

Fold a sheet of paper in half. Draw the front
half of an animal on one part. Draw the back
half of a different animal on the other part.
   Name your silly animal. Write a sentence
about it. Write the naming part on the first
half. Write the action part on the second half.

EXTRA! Cut your paper in half. Mix and match
silly animals with your classmates.

TV Poetry

Draw a TV set on a sheet of paper. Write a question about a TV show on the TV screen. Then write a telling sentence that answers the question. Make the sentences rhyme. Draw something from the TV show around the poem. You will have a TV poem.

Sentence Game

Players 2 or more

You need 4 note cards for each player
some paper

Write a spelling word on each card. Write <u>T</u> for telling sentence or <u>Q</u> for question.

How to play Mix the cards. Put them face down in a pile. Draw a card. Read the word and the letter <u>T</u> or <u>Q</u> out loud. Another player must write the word. Then the player must use it in a telling sentence or a question.

Scoring 1 point for each word spelled correctly
1 point for each correct sentence

Extra Practice: Unit 2

1 | What Is a Sentence? (page 37)

● ▲ Draw lines to make sentences.

★ The picture   crossed the sky.

1. Mary Anne   painted the picture.

2. The rainbow   were red and blue.

3. The colors   showed a rainbow.

■ Write the sentence part from the Word Box
that fits in each sentence.

John	kitten
barks	crawls

★ The dog _______ barks _______.

4. _________________ has a turtle.

5. His pet turtle _________________.

6. My _________________ has whiskers.

2 | Naming Part (page 39)

● ▲ Write a naming part from the Word Box to begin each sentence.

Chicks   Bees Birds   Frogs Lions

★ _Chicks_ peep.

1. _____________ leap.

2. _____________ sing.

3. _____________ sting.

4. _____________ roar.

■ Draw a line under each naming part.

★ <u>Those snakes</u> hiss.

5. Babies kiss.
6. Children skip.
7. Raindrops drip.
8. Most kittens play.
9. The goat eats hay.

10. Bears growl.
11. Those monkeys howl.
12. Roosters crow.
13. Some farmers hoe.
14. Cows moo and chew.

3 | Action Part (page 41)

● ▲ Write an action part from the Word Box to finish each sentence.

rolls	shines	spills	ring
chirps	bloom	runs	

★ The rabbit  *runs* .

1. The flowers __________ .

2. The sun __________ .

3. The robin __________ .

4. The ball __________ .

5. The bells __________ .

6. The milk __________ .

■ Add an action part to finish each sentence.

★ Flowers *grow in my garden* .

7. Bees __________ .

8. Birds __________ .

9. My dad and I __________ .

4 | Is It a Sentence? (page 43)

● ▲ Write **yes** before the sentences. Write **no**
before the words that are not sentences.

______ no ______ ★ a big park   ______ **2.** We ran home.

______ **1.** Children played.   ______ **3.** sat on swings

■ Draw lines to show the naming and action
parts. Put them together. Write the sentences.

★ love the rain. | naming part |

Sid and I | action part |

Sid and I love the rain.

4. We | naming part |

wear red boots. | action part |

____

5. fall on us. | naming part |

Big drops | action part |

____

5° | Telling Sentences (page 45)

●▲ Draw a line under each correct telling sentence.

★ <u>I have a fish.</u>

I have a fish

1. it lives in a fishbowl

It lives in a fishbowl.

2. the fish has blue stripes

The fish has blue stripes.

3. It is a zebra fish.

it is a zebra fish

4. i like my pet

I like my pet.

■ Write these telling sentences correctly.

★ Joe has a parrot

Joe has a parrot.

5. it has green wings

6. the parrot talks

7. it flies around the cage

6 | Questions (page 47)

● ▲ Draw a line under each correct question.

★ where is the puppy

<u>Where is the puppy?</u>

1. Is it under the bed?

is it under the bed?

2. did you call the puppy

Did you call the puppy?

3. Did you hear a bark?

did you hear a bark

4. is it in the back yard

Is it in the back yard?

■ Write the questions correctly.

★ do you have a pet

Do you have a pet?

5. Is it a duck

6. what is its name

7. can it swim

7 | Which Kind of Sentence? (page 49)

● ▲ Circle the **T** after each telling sentence.
Circle the **Q** after each question.

★ Do you like kittens?   T   (Q)

  1. Lee has a kitten.   T   Q
  2. Kittens are very nice.   T   Q
  3. Would you like one?   T   Q
  4. Dogs are good pets.   T   Q
  5. We have a pet bird.   T   Q
  6. Do you have a pet?   T   Q
  7. What color is your fish?   T   Q
  8. It is orange and black.   T   Q

■ Write these as sentences. Use capital letters and end marks correctly.

★ we walked in the woods

We walked in the woods.

9. it was in the fall

10. did you see the pretty leaves

11. what colors were they

Literature and Writing
A Story About Me

Why does Rosa want a new chair for her mother?

A Chair for My Mother

By Vera B. Williams

My mother works as a waitress in the Blue Tile Diner. After school sometimes I go to meet her there. Then her boss Josephine gives me a job too.

I wash the salts and peppers and fill the ketchups. One time I peeled all the onions for the onion soup. When I finish, Josephine says, ''Good work, honey,'' and pays me. And every time, I put half of my money into the jar.

It takes a long time to fill a jar this big. Every day when my mother comes home from work, I take down the jar. My mama empties all her change from tips out of her purse for me to count. Then we push all of the coins into the jar.

Sometimes my mama is laughing when she comes home from work. Sometimes she's so tired she falls asleep while I count the money out into piles. Some days she has lots of tips. Some days she has only a little. Then she looks worried. But each evening every single shiny coin goes into the jar.

We sit in the kitchen to count the tips. Usually Grandma sits with us too. While we count, she likes to hum. Often she has money in her old leather wallet for us. Whenever she gets a good bargain on tomatoes or bananas or something she buys, she puts by the savings and they go into the jar.

When we can't get a single other coin into the jar, we are going to take out all the money and go and buy a chair.

Yes, a chair. A wonderful, beautiful, fat, soft armchair. We will get one covered in velvet with roses all over it. We are going to get the best chair in the whole world.

That is because our old chairs burned up. There was a big fire in our other house. All our chairs burned. So did our sofa and so did everything else. That wasn't such a long time ago.

My mother and I were coming home from buying new shoes. I had new sandals. She had new pumps. We were walking to our house from the bus. We were looking at everyone's tulips. She

was saying she liked red tulips and I was saying
I liked yellow ones. Then we came to our block.

Right outside our house stood two big fire
engines. I could see lots of smoke. Tall orange
flames came out of the roof. All the neighbors
stood in a bunch across the street. Mama grabbed
my hand and we ran. My Uncle Sandy saw us and
ran to us. Mama yelled, "Where's Mother?" I
yelled, "Where's my grandma?" My Aunt Ida
waved and shouted, "She's here, she's here. She's
okay. Don't worry."

Grandma was all right. Our cat was safe too,
though it took a while to find her. But everything
else in our whole house was spoiled.

What was left of the house was turned to
charcoal and ashes.

We went to stay with my mother's sister Aunt
Ida and Uncle Sandy. Then we were able to move
into the apartment downstairs. We painted the
walls yellow. The floors were all shiny. But the
rooms were very empty.

The first day we moved in, the neighbors
brought dinner. And they brought a lot of other
things too.

The family across the street brought a table
and three kitchen chairs. The very old man next
door gave us a bed from when his children were
little.

My other grandpa brought us his beautiful rug.
My mother's other sister, Sally, had made us red
and white curtains. Mama's boss, Josephine,
brought pots and pans, silverware and dishes. My
cousin brought me her own stuffed bear.

Everyone clapped when my grandma made a
speech. "You are all the kindest people," she said,
"and we thank you very, very much. It's lucky
we're young and can start all over."

That was last year, but we still have no sofa
and no big chairs. When Mama comes home, her
feet hurt. "There's no good place for me to take
a load off my feet," she says. When Grandma
wants to sit back and hum and cut up potatoes,
she has to get as comfortable as she can on a
hard kitchen chair.

So that is how come Mama brought home the
biggest jar she could find at the diner and all the
coins started to go into the jar.

Now the jar is too heavy for me to lift down. Uncle Sandy gave me a quarter. He had to boost me up so I could put it in.

After supper Mama and Grandma and I stood in front of the jar. "Well, I never would have believed it, but I guess it's full," Mama said.

My mother brought home little paper wrappers for the nickels and the dimes and the quarters. I counted them all out and wrapped them all up.

On my mother's day off, we took all the coins to the bank. The bank exchanged them for ten-dollar bills. Then we took the bus downtown to shop for our chair.

We shopped through four furniture stores. We tried out big chairs and smaller ones, high chairs and low chairs, soft chairs and harder ones. Grandma said she felt like Goldilocks in "The Three Bears" trying out all the chairs.

Finally we found the chair we were all dreaming of. And the money in the jar was enough to pay for it. We called Aunt Ida and Uncle Sandy. They came right down in their pickup truck to drive the chair home for us. They knew we couldn't wait for it to be delivered.

I tried out our chair in the back of the truck. Mama wouldn't let me sit there while we drove.

But they let me sit in it while they carried it up to the door.

We set the chair right beside the window with the red and white curtains. Grandma and Mama and I all sat in it while Aunt Ida took our picture.

Now Grandma sits in it and talks with people going by in the daytime. Mama sits down and watches the news on TV when she comes home from her job. After supper, I sit with her and she can reach right up and turn out the light if I fall asleep in her lap.

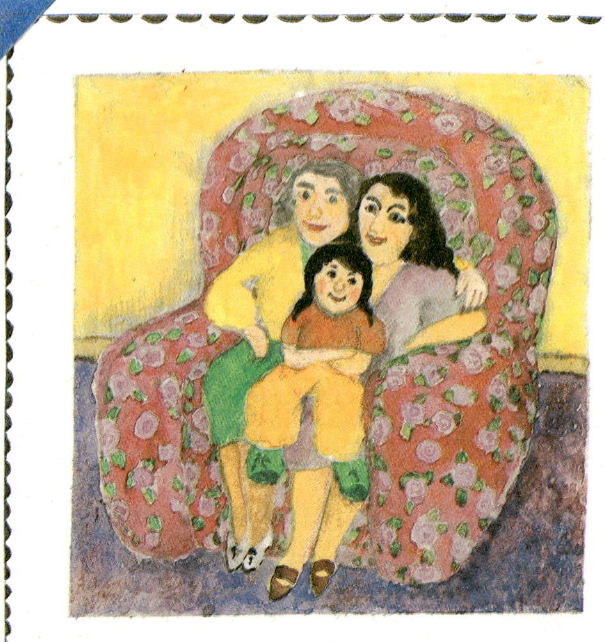

Think and Discuss

1. What happened to Rosa and her family about a year ago? Why did Rosa's mother need a new chair?

2. The people or animals in a story are called **characters.** Rosa and her mother are two characters in ''A Chair for My Mother.'' Who are some other characters in the story? Think about some of the things Rosa said and did. What kind of person is Rosa? her mother?

3. Why do you think Rosa and her family saved their money in a big glass jar? Would it have been better to put the money in a bank?

70

RESPONDING TO LITERATURE

The Reading and Writing Connection

Personal Response Would you like to buy something for a friend or for yourself? Write about something you would like to save for.

Creative Writing Rosa and her family have a beautiful new chair. What will they save for next? Write a story about the next thing they buy.

Creative Activities

Keep a Notebook Write your thoughts and ideas. Write about things that happen to you. You may want to use these ideas later for writing stories about yourself.

Tell a Story About Yourself Rosa told about buying a new chair. Tell your classmates about something you have done.

Vocabulary

Rosa's mother had a job as a waitress. What did she do? Name some other jobs. Make a jobs chart.

VOCABULARY CONNECTION

Compound Words

A **compound word** is made up of two words.

every + one = everyone

down + town = downtown

> Then we took the bus **downtown** to shop for our chair.
>
> from ''A Chair for My Mother'' by Vera B. Williams

Practice

Match the words to make compound words from ''A Chair for My Mother.''

★ arm   time

1. silver   stairs

2. day   ★ chair

3. down   ware

4. pick   up

Now write the compound words you made.

1. __________________   3. __________________

2. __________________   4. __________________

Listening and Speaking: Talking About Writing

You must listen carefully to a story before you can talk about it. Jed wrote this story and read it to Lee. Listen as your teacher reads it.

Now listen to what Jed and Lee said.

- What nice thing did Lee say about the story?
- What question did Lee ask?
- What new ideas can Jed add to his story?

Use these Speaking Helps when a friend asks you to help with a story.

Listening and Speaking Helps

1. Listen carefully.
2. Tell something you liked about the story or tell something you heard.
3. Ask questions if you do not understand.
4. Be polite.

Practice

With a partner listen to this story. Think of two questions to ask the writer. Then pretend to be the writer and answer the questions.

Thinking: Real and Pretend

Some things are real, and some are pretend. Some stories are about real life, and some are about make-believe people and animals. "A Chair for My Mother" is a story about real life. The characters and the things that happen are real.

Now read this story. Which parts could really happen? Which parts are pretend?

The Wind and the Sun

One day the sun and wind were arguing about who was stronger. They decided to have a contest.

A boy was walking down the street. He was wearing a coat.

"I will blow that boy's coat off," said the wind. "Then you will see that I am stronger than you!" The wind blew, but the boy just pulled his coat tighter.

"Now watch me," said the sun. He began to shine on the boy. The boy felt warm. He took off his coat.

"Well," said the sun to the wind, "I guess I really am stronger than you."

Which of these events in the story could not really happen?

The wind blows.   The sun and wind argue.

Thinking Helps

1. Stories are about real life or pretend life.
2. To help you decide, think of the people or events. Could they be real? Are they make-believe?

Practice

Which of these events could be real? Which of these events could be pretend? Write **R** in front of each real event. Write **P** in front of each pretend event.

__________ A house catches on fire.

__________ A wolf flies.

__________ A flower grows.

__________ A tree sings.

COMPOSITION SKILL

Telling About One Idea ☑

Jenny drew pictures after she read "A Chair for My Mother." She wanted to show how saving a little money each day could lead to a big beautiful chair. Which picture does not fit?

Jenny wrote to a friend about her new plan to save money for a trip. Which sentence does not fit?

> My mother and I are saving money in a jar for a trip. My mother puts all her extra change in the jar. I put half of what I earn in the jar too. I don't really like onions. Our jar is almost full, so soon we will go on our trip.

Prewriting Practice

A. Cross out the picture that does not fit.

1.

2.

3.

4.

B. Cross out the sentence that does not fit.

We found a lost dog in front of our school. We put a note about the dog on a tree. It said the dog was white with black spots. My cat is white with black spots too. The owner saw our note and came for her dog. We were sad to see the dog go.

Telling Enough ☑

In "A Chair for My Mother," Rosa told what happened when her family moved.

> The first day we moved in, the neighbors brought dinner. And they brought a lot of other things too.
>
> from "A Chair for My Mother" by Vera B. Williams

Then Rosa added these sentences.

> The family across the street brought a table and three kitchen chairs. The very old man next door gave us a bed from when his children were little.
>
> from "A Chair for My Mother" by Vera B. Williams

The second part gives a clearer picture. It tells about the neighbors and their gifts.

When you write a story, be like Rosa. Give a clear picture of what happened. Tell enough.

Prewriting Practice

Read this story. Do you think it tells enough?

> Monty was lost. My brother and I looked for him everywhere. We had no luck. Then we found him.

Who is Monty? Where did they look for him? Where did they find him? How did they feel?
Now fill in words to make the story tell enough.

____

My _________________________ Monty

was lost. My brother and I looked for him

____

in the _________________________

____

and under the _________________________.

We had no luck. Then we found him near the

____

____

____

When we saw him, we _________________________

____

____

_______________________________.

Step 1: Prewriting—Choose a Topic

Sandy thought about the special things she had done. She thought it would also be fun to write about these things. Sandy made this list.

> the snowman I made
>
> the time I was a clown
>
> my day at the fair

Sandy thought about each idea on her list. Which idea would make the best story?

the snowman I made

Maybe she would write about that.

the time I was a clown

That had been so long ago. Could she remember enough things about being a clown?

my day at the fair

That would be fun to tell about! She thought her class would like hearing about it too.

Sandy drew a picture of her day at the fair.
Then she showed her picture to Dan. She told
him all about her day. She told him about the
watermelon contest and the blue ribbon. She
told him about seeing prize sheep and eating
corn on the cob.

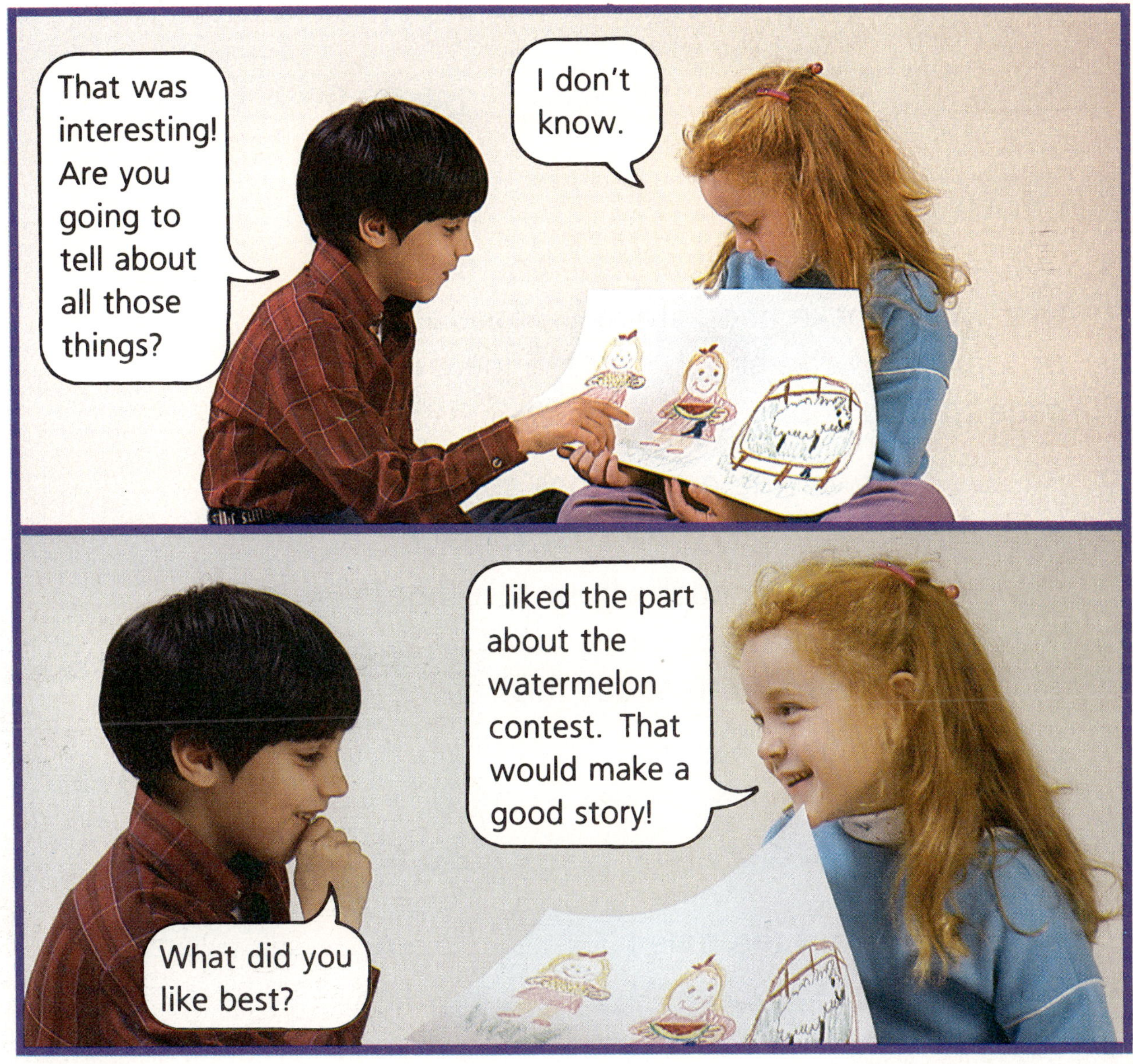

After talking with Dan, Sandy wrote this
sentence.

I will write about the contest
I won.

On Your Own

1. **Think** What special times have you had that would make good stories? Make a list of topics to write about. Use the Ideas page to help you.

2. **Choose** Answer these questions about each topic.

> Do I remember enough about this time?
> Is this topic about only one idea?
> Would I like to write about this?

Circle a topic from your list. Then finish this sentence.

I will write about the time I _______________________

____ .

3. **Try it** Draw a picture of your story. Show your picture to a partner. Tell your story. Then do the activity under "Thinking About Your Topic" on the Ideas page.

Ideas for Getting Started

Choosing Your Topic

Topic Ideas

My first day of school
Losing a front tooth
Meeting our new baby
My first time at camp

Getting Started

Ask yourself these questions. Do they give you any ideas?

What nice thing have I done for someone?
What funny thing has happened to me?

Thinking About Your Topic

WH Chart

Think about your topic. Who was there? What happened? Make a WH chart like Sandy's about your topic. Here is Sandy's chart.

My Day at the Fair

WHO?
me

WHAT?
watermelon contest
blue ribbon

WHERE?
at the fair

Step 2: Write a First Draft

Sandy thought about what to say in her story. Then she wrote her first draft. She did not worry about mistakes.

Sandy's first draft

> I was in a watermelon contest. ~~I ate~~ I gobbled up my piece as fast as i could. It was a mess. I won the blew ribbon!

Think and Discuss ☑

- What one idea is the story about?
- What else would you like to know?
- Why did Sandy use <u>gobbled</u> instead of <u>ate</u>?

On Your Own

1. **Ask yourself** Think about what you want
to say. Answer these questions.

> What did I see and do?
> How did I feel—happy? sad? scared?
> What will interest other people?

2. **Write your first draft** Do not worry about
mistakes. You can make changes later.

Step 3: Revise

Sandy read over her story. She added a
sentence to make it better.

Then she read her story to Rosa. Did
Rosa give Sandy any new ideas?

Reading and responding

Sandy made changes, using Rosa's ideas.
Read Sandy's revised story on the next page.

> I was in a watermelon contest.
> The judge said, "Get ready. Go!"
> ~~I ate~~ I gobbled up my piece as
> fast as i could. ~~It was a mess.~~
> I won the blew ribbon!
> My hands and face were sticky,
> but I didn't care.

Think and Discuss ☑

- Which sentence did Sandy cross out? Why?
- Which sentences did she add? Why?

On Your Own

Revising checklist

☑ Did I tell enough about what happened?

☑ Do all my sentences fit?

1. **Revise** Cross out sentences that do not tell about your topic. Add words that tell more about what happened.

2. **Have a conference** Read your story to a classmate. What else would your classmate like to know? Make any changes that will make your story clearer.

See the Thesaurus on page 347.

Step 4: Proofread

Sandy proofread her story. She checked for mistakes and corrected them.

Sandy's story after proofreading

I was in a watermelon contest.
The judge said, "Get ready. Go!"
I ate I gobbled up my piece as
fast as i could. It was a mess.
blue
I won the blew ribbon!
My hands and face were sticky,
but I didn't care.

Think and Discuss
- Which word needed a capital letter?
- Which word was not spelled correctly?

1. **Proofreading Practice** There are two mistakes in each sentence. Write the sentences correctly.

   a. did I tell you my story.

   b. I missed the skool bus?

   c. i ran two whole miles

2. **Proofread** Proofread your story. Use the checklist and proofreading marks to help you.

Proofreading Checklist	Proofreading Marks
☑ **1.** Did I begin each sentence with a capital letter?	∧ Add
☑ **2.** Did I use correct end marks?	— Take out
☑ **3.** Did I spell each word correctly?	≡ Make a capital letter ／ Make a small letter

The Grammar/Spelling Connection

Grammar Helps
- A sentence begins with a capital letter.
- A question ends with a question mark.

Spelling Help
- The short **e** sound may be spelled <u>e</u>. (p<u>e</u>t)

Step 5: Publish

Sandy copied her story very neatly. She checked it again and added a title. How did Sandy make her story look special?

On Your Own

1. **Copy** Copy your story carefully. Check it.

2. **Add a title** Write a title for your story.

3. **Share** Read and show your story to your class or to someone at home.

Idea for Sharing

Draw an outline of something from your story. Cut out what you have drawn. Paste your story onto it.

Applying A Story About Me

Writing Across the Curriculum
Math

It is fun to use numbers. You can count. You can tell how old you are. Can you write a story about yourself, using numbers? Here are some ideas. Follow the five writing steps.

1. **Go shopping.** Look at the picture. What would you buy with two dollars? Write a story about your shopping trip.

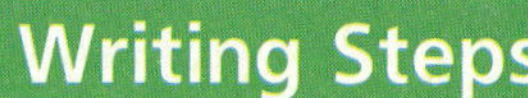

2. **Tell about time.** These clocks show different times. Write a story about your day and what you do at these times. You may want to use words in the Word Bank.

Tammy read "A Chair for My Mother." She liked reading about families. Next, she read a book called <u>I Love Gram</u> by Ruth Sonneborn. Tammy wrote this book report to share with her class.

The title is <u>I Love Gram.</u>

The author is <u>Ruth Sonneborn.</u>

This book is about <u>a little girl and her grandmother. Ellie's grandmother got sick and went to the hospital. Ellie missed her grandmother a lot. Then Ellie got good news. Gram was coming home!</u>

I think this book <u>is good. I liked it because Gram and Ellie loved each other. Ellie made Gram a special coming-home surprise.</u>

Think and Discuss
- What is the title? Who is the author?
- What is this book about?
- Why did Tammy like this book?

Share Your Book

Write a Book Report

1. Copy the form on page 92.
2. Write the title of your book. Draw a line under it.
3. Write the name of the author.
4. Write what the book is about.
5. Write what you think of the book.
6. Share your book report with your class.

The Book Nook

Music, Music for Everyone	Timothy and Gramps
by Vera B. Williams	by Ron Brooks
Grandma helps Rosa learn to play the accordion.	Timothy likes school better after Gramps visits his classroom.

Language and Usage
Nouns

1 | Naming Words

Some words name people.

The **man** walks.

The **girl** runs.

Which words name people? A word that names a person is called a **noun.**

Guided Practice Tell which words are nouns.

★ The girl hides.   girl

1. The mother smiles.
2. A boy looks.
3. The baby laughs.

Now write the nouns.

1. _______________   2. _______________   3. _______________

Summing up

▶ A word that names a person is called a **noun.**

★ The girl has a birthday.

The girl has a birthday.

1. The father serves food.

2. The sister plays music.

3. The mother sings a song.

4. The brother carries gifts.

5. A friend helps.

Writing Application: Descriptions
Write about how people help you. Use the
words doctor, dentist, teacher, and police
officer.

For Extra Practice, see p. 116.

2 | More Naming Words

You know that a noun names a person. A noun can also name a place or a thing.

Tom went to the lake.

Did he see the big fish?

Which noun names a place? Which noun names a thing?

Guided Practice Read the sentences. Tell which words are nouns that name places and things.

★ We went to the farm.   farm

1. Dan drove the truck.   **3.** We saw a horse.

2. The barn was huge.   **4.** I dug up a carrot.

Now write the nouns.

1. _______________________   3. _______________________

2. _______________________   4. _______________________

Summing up

▶ A noun names a person, a place, or a thing.

Independent Practice

A. Write the sentences. Draw a line under
each noun that names a place or a thing.

★ Do you have a baseball?

<u>Do you have a baseball?</u>

1. We could play at school.

2. My glove is new.

3. We can go to the park.

B. Draw a line under the noun in each row.

★ over   grow   <u>shoe</u>

4. home   keep   give

5. ask   shirt   fell

6. long   tell   library

Writing Application: Creative Writing
Pretend that you are going to live in a jungle.
Write about the things you would take with
you and why.

For Extra Practice, see p. 117.

3 | One and More Than One

You have learned that a noun can name one person, place, or thing. A noun can also name more than one person, place, or thing.

Which noun names one? Which noun names more than one? What letter was added? Most nouns add <u>s</u> to name more than one.

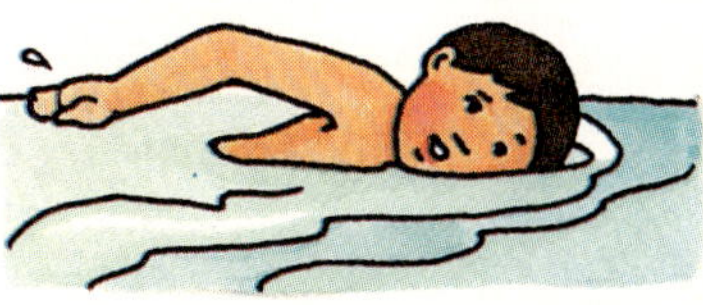

swimmer

swimmers

Guided Practice Tell which nouns name more than one.

★ The <u>teams</u> will have a <u>race</u>. teams

1. The <u>swimmers</u> are at the <u>side</u>.
2. The <u>bells</u> by the <u>pool</u> ring.
3. The <u>racers</u> dive into the <u>water</u>.
4. The <u>winner</u> gets <u>prizes</u>.

Now write the nouns that name more than one.

1. _______________________ 3. _______________________

2. _______________________ 4. _______________________

Summing up

▶ Add <u>s</u> to most nouns to name more than one.

Independent Practice

A. Draw a line under each noun that names more than one. Then write the sentences.

★ The (sock, <u>socks</u>) are green.

The socks are green.

1. The (coat, coats) are warm.

2. The (hats, hat) look pretty.

3. The (girls, girl) are ready to go.

B. Write each noun to name more than one.

★ hat 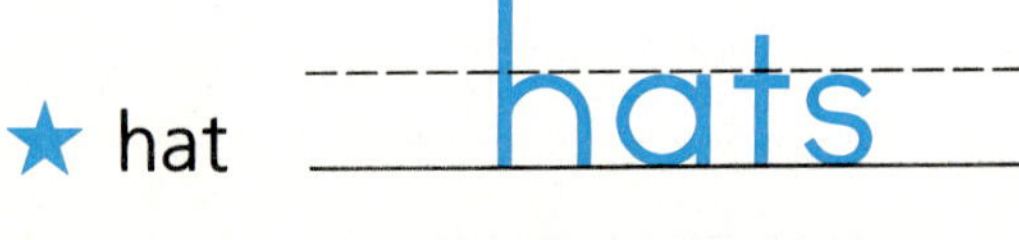

5. boat

4. shirt

6. book

Writing Application: Description

Write about things you like to play with, such as dolls or baseballs. Use nouns ending with <u>s</u>.

For Extra Practice, see p. 118.

4 | Adding es

Some nouns add <u>s</u> to name more than one. Other nouns add <u>es</u>. Words that end with <u>s</u>, <u>x</u>, <u>ch</u>, and <u>sh</u> add <u>es</u> to name more than one.

class	class**es**	bench	bench**es**
box	box**es**	dish	dish**es**

dress

Guided Practice Tell which nouns name more than one.

★ I found old (glass, glasses).   glasses

1. Maria can wear these (dress, dresses).
2. Roberto has two gold (watches, watch).
3. Here are some blue (dishes, dish).

Now write the sentences correctly.

1. ____

2. ____

3. ____

dresses

Summing up

▶ Add <u>es</u> to nouns that end in <u>x</u>, <u>ch</u>, <u>sh</u>, or <u>s</u> to name more than one.

Independent Practice

A. Draw a line under each noun that names more than one. Then write the sentences.

★ The (fox, <u>foxes</u>) play here.

The foxes play here.

1. They hide in the (bushes, bush).

2. Did you bring our (lunches, lunch)?

3. Where are the (peach, peaches)?

B. Write each noun to name more than one.

★ six   *sixes*   **6.** bus

4. brush

7. fox

5. beach

8. bunch

Writing Application: A Story
Write a story about two foxes that get lost.

For Extra Practice, see p. 119.

5 | Nouns That Change Spelling

You know that most nouns add <u>s</u> or <u>es</u> to name more than one. A few nouns change their spelling to name more than one.

child   **children**   man   **men**   woman   **women**

Which nouns name more than one?

Guided Practice Name each picture.

   women

Now write the nouns.

1. _______________________   2. _______________________

Summing up

▶ Some nouns change spelling to name more than one.

Independent Practice

A. Draw a line under the noun that fits each sentence. Then write the sentences.

★ Two (child, <u>children</u>) yelled.

Two children yelled.

1. Some (woman, women) saw a donkey.

2. Three (man, men) chased the donkey.

3. Two (woman, women) stopped it.

B. Write each noun to name more than one.

★ child 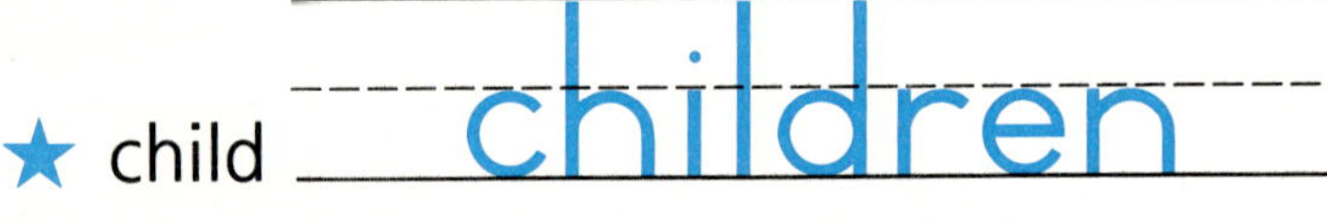 children

4. man ________________________ **5.** woman ______________________

Writing Application: A Story
Write a story about the people in a town. Use the words <u>men</u>, <u>women</u>, and <u>children</u>. Tell what they like to do.

For Extra Practice, see p. 120.

6 | Special Nouns

Some nouns name special people, places, or things. These special nouns begin with capital letters.

Nouns	Special Nouns
man	**D**ean
street	**E**lm **S**treet
town	**L**akewood
pet	**W**ags

Guided Practice Tell which nouns are special nouns. They need capital letters.

★ My brother sam tells funny jokes.   Sam

1. I have a friend named ned.
2. He lives in farwell.
3. His kitten is called fluffy.
4. He has a sister named carol.

Now write the special nouns correctly.

1. ______________________   3. ______________________

2. ______________________   4. ______________________

Summing up

▶ Begin the names of special people, places, and things with capital letters.

A. Write the special nouns correctly.

★ Where is eric today?

1. He went to denver.

2. He took his dog woof.

B. Write the sentences correctly.

★ My friend sue visits me.

3. She lives on east street.

4. It is in portland.

5. Her cat is named harry.

Writing Application: About Myself
Write about yourself. Tell your name. Name
your sisters, brothers, pets, and town.

For Extra Practice, see p. 121.

7 | Words for Nouns

You know that a noun names a person, a place, or a thing. A **pronoun** is a word that can take the place of a noun. Which pronouns take the place of the nouns?

Now the plane lands.   Now it lands.
Emily looks out.   She looks out.
Jeff stands up.   He stands up.
Jeff and Emily leave.   They leave.

Guided Practice Tell which pronoun in the Word Box can take the place of the underlined word or words in each sentence.

★ Mother makes great bread.   She

1. Steve and Betsy made bread.
2. Betsy warmed some milk.
3. Steve added flour.
4. The bread was soon done.

They	It
She	He

Now write the correct pronoun for each sentence.

1. __________ 2. __________ 3. __________ 4. __________

Summing up

▶ A **pronoun** can take the place of a noun. They, he, she, and it are pronouns.

Independent Practice Write each sentence. Use the pronoun from the Word Box that fits the underlined word or words.

They	It	She	He

★ <u>Tom</u> started the washer.

He started the washer.

1. <u>Lucy</u> added soap.

2. <u>The washer</u> washed the clothes.

3. <u>Tom</u> washed the dishes.

4. <u>Tom and Lucy</u> put the dishes away.

5. <u>The house</u> looked clean.

Writing Application: Description
Write about a game. Use <u>he</u>, <u>she</u>, <u>it</u>, and <u>they</u>.

For Extra Practice, see p. 122.

8 | Naming Yourself Last

When you talk about someone else and yourself, name yourself last.

Tina and I rode our new bikes.

Guided Practice Tell how to make the sentences correct.

★ I and Ann played. Ann and I played.

1. I and Carl ran a race.
2. I and Amy jumped rope.
3. I and Molly made kites.
4. I and Sid walked home.

Now write the sentences correctly.

1. ______________________________

2. ______________________________

3. ______________________________

4. ______________________________

Summing up

▶ When you talk about another person and yourself, name yourself last.

Independent Practice Write the
sentences correctly.

★ I and Jane paint.

Jane and I paint.

1. I and Jed sing songs.

2. I and Liz write letters.

3. I and Bob go fishing.

4. I and Lynn like animals.

5. I and Lou ice-skate.

6. I and Stan ride horses.

Writing Application: A Story
Write a story about something you did with a
friend. Use your friend's name and the word I.

For Extra Practice, see p. 123.

Grammar-Writing Connection

Writing Clearly with Nouns

Nouns name persons, places, and things. Writers carefully choose nouns that give the most information and details. Which sentence below tells you more?

> The child walked to school.

> The boy walked to Lakeville School.

The second sentence tells you more. Using exact nouns makes your writing more interesting.

Revising Sentences

Change the underlined noun in each sentence to give more information. Write your new noun.

★ The <u>man</u> cut my hair. 

1. The <u>animal</u> escaped. 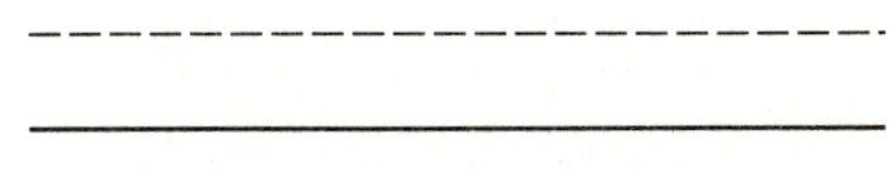

2. The <u>thing</u> tickled me.

3. The <u>lady</u> wore a crown. 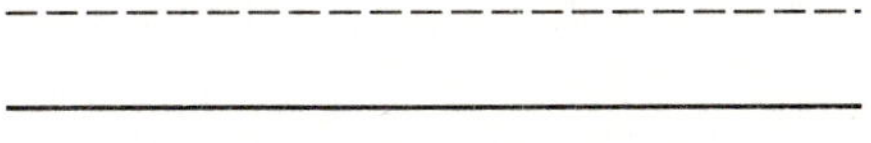

4. My father cooked <u>food</u>. 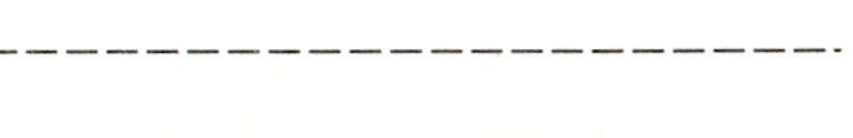

Grammar-Writing Connection

Creative Writing

Still Life with Puppies (1888)
by Paul Gauguin
The Museum of
Modern Art
New York

Can you find the three puppies? Paul Gauguin has painted them from up above.

- What other things are in the picture?

Activities

1. **Write a letter.** Pretend that these are your puppies. Write a letter about them.
2. **Write a story.** Write a story that one puppy might tell about the three puppies.

Check-up: Unit 4

Naming Words (pages 95, 97)

Draw a line under each noun that names a person, a place, or a thing.

1. The lake was pretty.   **3.** My father cooked.

2. The camper was warm.

One and More Than One (page 99)

Draw a line under each noun that names more than one.

4. Three (boat, boats) went by.

5. We sat on some (blankets, blanket).

6. I read some (book, books).

Adding es (page 101)

Write each noun to name more than one.

7. dish _______________   **9.** fox _______________

8. bus _______________   **10.** lunch _______________

Nouns That Change Spelling (page 103)

Write each noun to name more than one.

11. child _______________   **13.** woman _______________

12. man _______________

Special Nouns (page 105)
Write each special noun correctly.

14. My sister is called maggie.

15. She has a dog named duke.

16. We live in newton.

17. Our house is on oak road.

Words for Nouns (page 107)
Draw a line under the pronoun that can take the place of the underlined word or words.

18. Jenny and Paul hiked up the hill.

    It   She   They

19. The top was very high.

    He   They   It

20. Jenny could see very far.

    She   They   He

Naming Yourself Last (page 109)
Draw a line under the correct words.

21. (Lee and I, I and Lee) run races.

22. (I and Ed, Ed and I) sail boats.

23. (I and Nan, Nan and I) read books.

Enrichment

Using Nouns

Picture Names

Cut out a picture from a magazine. Paste it on a sheet of paper. Write the names of all the people, places, and things in the picture on the back.

Trade pictures with a classmate. Make a list for your classmate's picture. (Do not peek at your classmate's list first!) Then look at the back. Did you both write the same words?

Address Book

Make a book with three sheets of paper. Write a friend's name on each page. Draw a picture of the friend. Then write a sentence about your friend under the picture. Write the name of the street where your friend lives.

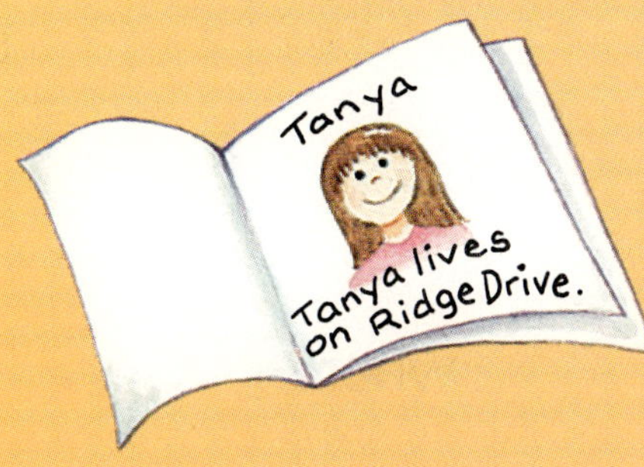

EXTRA! Use the telephone book. Add your friends' telephone numbers to your address book.

1 | Naming Words (page 95)

●▲ Draw a line under each word that names a person. Write the word.

★ A <u>dancer</u> leaped.   dancer

1. The teacher watched.

2. A man played music.

3. One student practiced.

4. All the people clapped.

■ Read the words. Draw a line from the Noun Box to each noun that names a person.

mother   under   friend

★ doctor   uncle   looking

boy

baker   drive

playmate   where

nurse   girl

father   dentist

2 | More Naming Words (page 97)

● ▲ Write each noun that names a place or a thing.

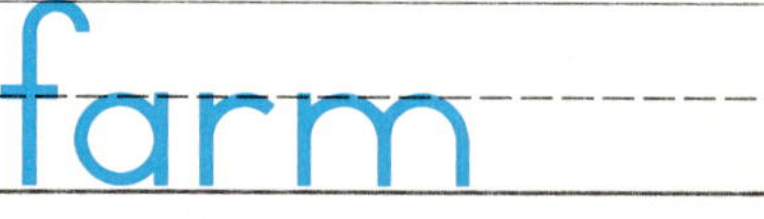

★ We went to a farm.

1. We looked at an old house.

2. We saw a huge field.

3. The corn grew tall.

4. The hay smelled sweet.

■ Draw a line under the noun in each row.

★	take	glass	sit
5.	go	like	silk
6.	town	eat	earn
7.	send	football	over
8.	week	save	hear
9.	see	street	live
10.	three	late	earth
11.	egg	brown	was

3 | One and More Than One (page 99)

●▲ Draw a line under each noun that names more than one.

★ We have two (garden, <u>gardens</u>).

1. Many (<u>plants</u>, plant) grow there.
2. One garden has (vegetable, <u>vegetables</u>).
3. The other one has (<u>flowers</u>, flower).
4. Chris and Rob plant (tulip, <u>tulips</u>).
5. Lisa grows (<u>carrots</u>, carrot).
6. Does your garden have (weed, <u>weeds</u>)?

■ Write each noun to name more than one.

★ car   *cars*

7. desk

8. clock

9. pencil

10. chair

11. picture

4 | Adding _es_ (page 101)

● ▲ Draw a line under each noun that names more
than one.

★ The (box, <u>boxes</u>) were stacked.

1. The workers ate their (lunch, lunches).
2. They painted two (bench, benches).
3. They painted three (porch, porches).
4. Then they cleaned all the (brush, brushes).

■ Write each noun to name more than one.

★ one bus   two ___buses___

5. one box   two __________

6. one dish   five __________

7. one patch   three __________

8. one watch   two __________

9. one glass   six __________

10. one circus   four __________

5 | Nouns That Change Spelling (p. 103)

● ▲ Draw a line under the noun that fits in each sentence.

★ All the (child, <u>children</u>) watched the game.

1. Today two (man, men) played tennis.
2. Another (man, men) kept score.
3. Four (woman, women) played later.
4. Some (child, children) will play tomorrow.

■ Write the word from the Word Box that fits in each sentence.

| man |
| men |

★ Two of my teachers are ___ men ___.

| man |
| men |

5. My art teacher is a ____________.

| child |
| children |

6. The ________________ like art class.

| child |
| children |

7. One ____________ wants to be an artist.

| woman |
| women |

8. Men and ________________ are artists.

6 | Special Nouns (p. 105)

● ▲ Draw a line under each special noun.
Then write each one correctly.

★ We moved to <u>elm lane</u>.

1. We live in wilton.

2. My new friend is benny.

3. His pony is named blaze.

■ Write the sentences correctly.

★ My pen pal is john.

4. His last name is singer.

5. He lives in dallas.

6. He has a fish named goldie.

7 | Words for Nouns (page 107)

● ▲ Read each sentence. Draw a line under the pronoun that can take the place of the underlined word or words.

★ <u>Stan</u> drove his sports car.

<u>He</u>   They   It

1. <u>Mary</u> went with him.

She   He   It

2. <u>The car</u> had a flat tire.

He   She   It

3. <u>Stan and Mary</u> fixed it.

It   They   He

■ Write each sentence, using a pronoun from the Word Box to replace the underlined words.

He	She	It	They

★ <u>Raul and Maria</u> visited me.

They visited me.

4. <u>Maria</u> enjoyed the visit.

____

5. <u>Raul</u> wrote a thank-you note.

____

8 | Naming Yourself Last (page 109)

● ▲ Draw a line under the words that fit in the sentences correctly.

★ (I and Andy, <u>Andy and I</u>) go fishing.

1. (Kate and I, I and Kate) ice-skate.

2. (I and Sue, Sue and I) play ball.

3. (Jack and I, I and Jack) collect stamps.

4. (I and Robin, Robin and I) go swimming.

5. (Carmen and I, I and Carmen) ride bikes.

6. (Mario and I, I and Mario) hike.

■ Circle the three sentences that are not correct. Write them correctly.

★ I and Doug go shopping.

Doug and I go shopping.

I and Willie are friends.
I and my sister like horses.
Sarah and I play the piano.

Ben and I will go to the fair.
I and Paulo have pet birds.

7. _______________________________________

8. _______________________________________

9. _______________________________________

Reeling in my kite
one day, I found
that I had caught a cloud.
Richard García
from ''Curb Your Cloud''

How does Nobody change Sarah's feelings about a terrible day?

Nobody

By Patience Brewster

Once there was a little girl named Sarah, who sometimes had terrible, good-for-nothing days. She had one of those days just a week before her birthday. Nothing had gone right, and by the time she came home from school, Sarah was very grumpy.

Mother took one look at her and said, "Sarah, who are you frowning at?"

"Nobody," mumbled Sarah.

"Well," said Mother, "tell me about school today. Who passed out the crackers at snack time?"

"Nobody," grumbled Sarah.

Mother thought for a minute. Then she said, "If Nobody passed out the crackers, then Nobody spilled the crackers, so Nobody had to pick them up. That Nobody must have been very busy today."

Sarah scowled. Then she began to smile as she imagined a funny Nobody doing all those things.

"What does Nobody look like?" asked Mother. "Can you draw me a picture?"

Sarah got out her best pencil and a big piece of paper. This is the picture she drew.

After that, Nobody was with Sarah all the time.

On Saturday, who do you suppose came to play with Sarah? Nobody. Sarah told Nobody stories and sang to Nobody. She had a teaparty and Nobody was invited.

On Sunday, Sarah looked all over the house for her doll Ellis. Nobody had hidden her, so Sarah found Ellis right where she had left her.

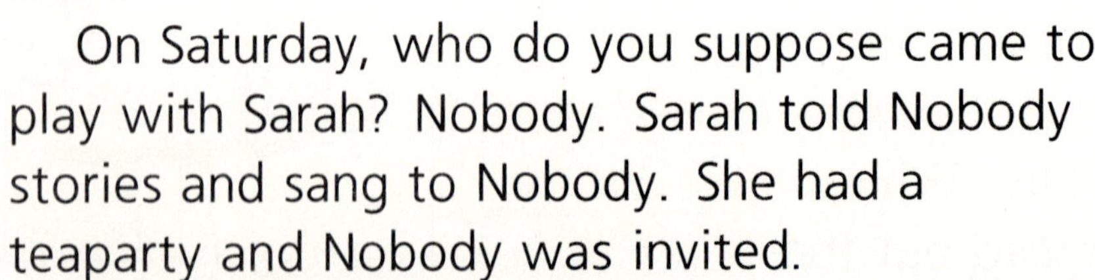

On Monday, who waited for the school bus with Sarah? Nobody. While Sarah waited, she had Nobody to talk to.

On Tuesday, Miss Fosdick said, ''Nobody is sick today.'' All the children cheered except Sarah. She felt sorry for Nobody. How would you feel if everyone was glad you were sick?

On Wednesday, Sarah bumped her elbow. It hurt and she started to cry. Father said, ''Listen. Who's crying?''

Sarah listened quietly. Who do you suppose was crying then? Nobody, of course.

On Thursday, Sarah was in a hurry. She left her room a mess. Guess who helped her clean up when she came home from school?

Nobody.

On Friday, when Sarah was tucked into bed
for the night, she heard funny noises. She
thought she saw the curtain move. But Sarah
wasn't frightened. She knew Nobody was
there.

Saturday was Sarah's birthday. Her friends
brought her some very nice presents. It was a
wonderful party. After everyone had gone
home, Sarah looked at all her new things and
noticed a gift that Nobody had wrapped. She
opened it up, and guess what . . .?

Nobody was inside!

Sarah was very happy.
Now Nobody really was
somebody.

Think and Discuss

1. How does Sarah feel at the beginning of the
   story? Why do her feelings change?

2. Was <u>Nobody</u> a good name for Sarah's
   special friend? Why do you think so?

3. "Nobody" is a **fiction** story. The author
   made up the story and the characters. What
   other fiction stories have you read?

RESPONDING TO LITERATURE

The Reading and Writing Connection

Personal Response Write why you would or would not like to have a friend like Nobody.

Creative Writing What else might have happened in the story "Nobody"? Write about something else that Sarah might do with Nobody.

Creative Activities

Make Story Puppets Make stick puppets of Sarah and Nobody. Take turns with a classmate acting out the story. What would Sarah and Nobody say to each other?

Your Own Nobody Look at the picture Sarah drew of Nobody. Now draw your own picture of Nobody. Share it with your class.

Vocabulary

The meanings of <u>nobody</u> and <u>somebody</u> are very different. They are opposites. Read these words from the story. Write the opposite of each one.

    sick   opened   grumpy   inside

VOCABULARY CONNECTION

Opposites

Words whose meanings are very different are
opposites.

> Now **Nobody** was really **somebody.**
>
> from "Nobody" by Patience Brewster

Practice

A. Find the opposites in each sentence. Draw
lines under them.

★ Sarah <u>scowled</u>, but then she <u>smiled</u>.

1. Sarah got a big piece of paper and drew
a little picture.

2. Sarah lost Ellis, but she found her again.

B. Write the word in the Word Box that is the
opposite of each word.

laugh	noisily	light	happy

★ grumpy _happy_   **2.** quietly ____

1. cry ____   **3.** heavy ____

130

Prewriting
Story

Listening: Story Order

A story tells what happens in a certain order. That way the story makes sense. Listen as your teacher reads from the story "Nobody."

When did Sarah have a "good-for-nothing day"? Was she grumpy before or after school?

Use these helps when you listen for order.

Listening Helps

1. Try to picture what happens. Does the order make sense?
2. Listen for clues about when something happens.

Practice

Listen as your teacher reads. Listen for when things happen. Number the pictures in order.

Speaking: Telling a Story

In "Nobody" the author tells what happened. She also tells you what the characters said.

When you tell a story, you can make it interesting by doing both those things.

Speaking Helps

1. Try to get your listener to enjoy your story.
2. Use words that show the characters. Choose words to help your listeners see the characters, the actions, and the place where the story happens.
3. Change your voice for different characters.
4. Use your voice to show different feelings.
5. Practice telling your story. Speak loudly and clearly.

Practice

In the story "Nobody," Sarah had a terrible day. Plan a story about a terrible day for you. Follow the Helps above. Tell your story to a friend.

Thinking: Putting Events in Order ☑

The author of "Nobody" used the days of the week to put the events in order. On Saturday Nobody played with Sarah. On Sunday Nobody hid Ellis, Sarah's doll.

One way to make order clear is to use order words.

first	before	after
next	then	finally

Thinking Helps

1. Think about why things happened in the order they did.
2. Think of words that help tell the order.

Practice

Number these events in an order that makes sense. Then write an order word for each event.

Sarah opened her presents.   ____   ________________

Sarah put on her birthday dress.   ____   ________________

Sarah's friends came to her party.   ____   ________________

Sarah's friends went home.   ____   ________________

COMPOSITION SKILL

Parts of a Story 

A story has a **beginning,** a **middle,** and an **end.** The beginning tells who is in a story and what it is about. The middle tells what happens. The end tells how the story works out.

beginning	middle	end

- What does the beginning of "Nobody" tell?
- What happens in the middle?
- How does "Nobody" end?

Prewriting Practice

Draw a middle for this story on another piece of paper.

The Writing Process
How to Write a Story

Step 1: Prewriting—Choose a Topic

Todd wanted to write a story for his sister. He made a list of ideas. Then he thought about each idea on his list.

the time I found a ring

This idea was for a story about himself. It was not make-believe.

a lost dog

Todd could not think of enough to say about this idea.

a boy looking for a pot of gold

Todd's father had once joked about a pot of gold at the end of a rainbow. That would make a good story!

Todd wrote these sentences.

I will write a story about a boy named Jason. He looks for a pot of gold at the end of a rainbow.

Todd drew a picture of Jason climbing a
rainbow. He showed his picture to a classmate.

On Your Own

1. **Think** What ideas do you have for
make-believe stories? List your ideas. Use
the Ideas page to help you.

2. **Choose** Answer these questions about
each idea.

> Is this an idea for a make-believe story?
> Can I think of enough to say?
> Would other people like this story?

Circle an idea from your list. Then finish
this sentence.

I will write a story about _______________

3. **Try it** What will you write? Do one of the
activities under "Thinking About Your Topic"
on the Ideas page.

Ideas for Getting Started

Choosing Your Topic

Topic Ideas

My life as a shoe   The polka dot puppy

Story Starters

What if giraffes could talk? What if you could travel on a flying carpet? Make a ''What if'' list of story ideas.

Thinking About Your Topic

Draw Your Story

Draw a block story about your topic. Show what will happen in the beginning, the middle, and the end. Set up your block story like this.

MY BLOCK STORY

beginning	middle	end

Talk About It

Tell a friend about your story idea. What else does your friend want to know?

Step 2: Write a First Draft

Todd was ready to write his first draft. He just wanted to get his ideas written down. He did not worry about mistakes.

Read Todd's first draft.

Todd's first draft

Once there was a boy named Jason. He met a funny man. ~~The man had a garden.~~ The man said there was a pot of gold at the end of a rainbow. ~~So he~~ One day Jason climbed a rainbow and walked and walked to the end. There was no pot of gold. Jason was mad! He went home.

Think and Discuss ☑
- What other endings could Todd's story have?
- Why did Todd cross out some words?

On Your Own

1. **Ask yourself** Think about what you want to write. Answer these questions.

   How will my story begin?
   What will happen in the middle?
   How will my story end?

2. **Write** Be sure your story has a beginning, a middle, and an end. Do not worry about mistakes. You can make changes later.

Step 3: Revise

Todd read his story. He thought something else should happen, but he did not know what.

Todd read his story to Maryanne. Maryanne liked Todd's idea. She thought something else should happen too.

Reading and responding

Todd thought of another idea. He crossed out his ending. He added more to the story. Read Todd's revised story on the next page.

Todd's revised story

Once there was a boy named Jason. He met a funny man. ~~The man had a garden.~~ The man said there was a pot of gold at the end of a rainbow. ~~So he~~ One day Jason climbed a rainbow and walked and walked to the end. There was no pot of gold. Jason was mad! ~~He went home.~~

Then the rainbow went away. Jason started to cry. An eegel heard him. it got him some crayons. "Get on my back," said the eegel. The eegel flew into the sky. Jason colored a new rainbow. He climbed down the rainbow and went home.

Think and Discuss ☑

- Which sentence did Todd cross out? Why?
- What ideas did Todd add to his story?

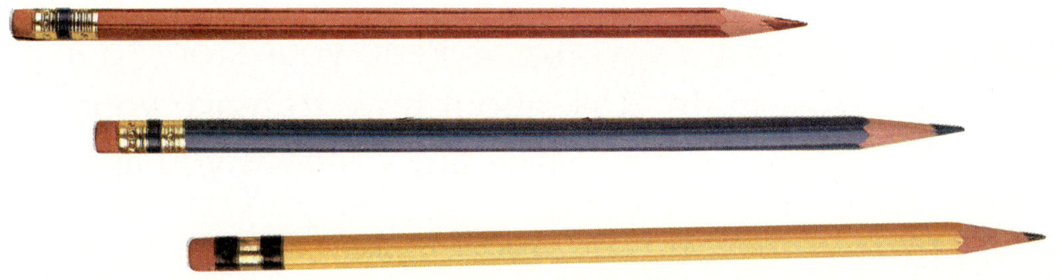

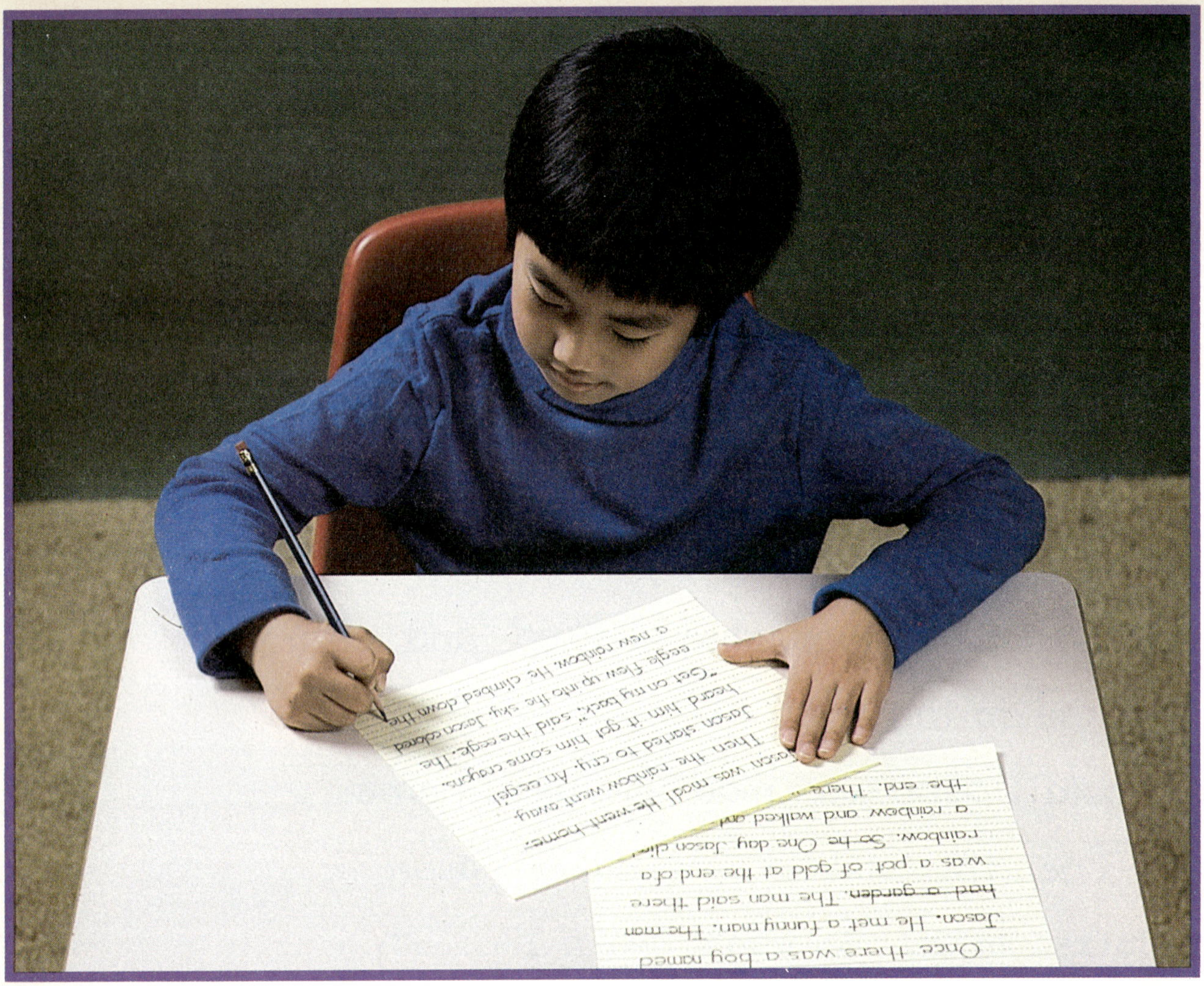

On Your Own

Revising checklist

☑ Are the events in the right order?

☑ Does it have a beginning, a middle, and an end?

1. **Revise** Write another ending. Use the new ending if you like it better. Cross out any sentences that are not needed. Add new words or sentences that you like.

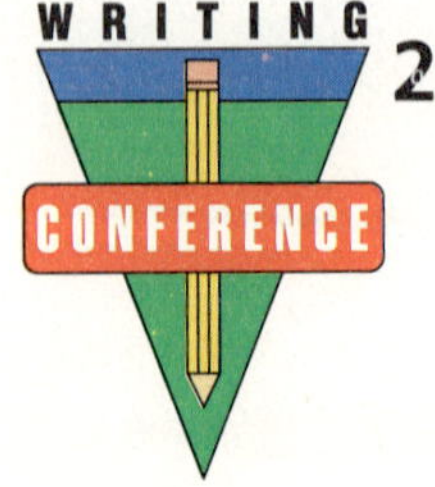

2. **Have a conference** Read your story to a classmate. Talk about how to make your story clearer. Make any changes you like.

See the Thesaurus on page 347.

Step 4: Proofread

Todd was ready to proofread his story. He checked for capital letters and end marks. He checked spellings in a dictionary.

Part of Todd's proofread story

> Then the rainbow went away. Jason started to cry. An ~~eegel~~ *eagle* heard him. <u>i</u>t got him some crayons. "Get on my back," said the ~~eegel~~ *eagle*. The ~~eegel~~ *eagle* flew into the sky. Jason colored a new rainbow. He climbed down the rainbow and went home.

Think and Discuss

- Which word was not spelled correctly?
- Which letter did he correct? Why?

1. Proofreading Practice Find two mistakes in each sentence. Check for correct end marks and for capital letters. Be sure all words are spelled correctly. Write each sentence correctly.

a. I and Tina moved to a new house

b. tina and i played in the green grass.

c. We mad plans for a garden

d. I and she loved the lak.

e. do you like the country.

f. we sleep under the stars?

144   **The Writing Process**

g. Tina and i shar a room.

____

- -

____

h. do you have your own room.

____

- -

____

2. **Proofread** Proofread your story. Use the checklist and proofreading marks to help you.

Proofreading Checklist
☑ **1.** Did I begin and end each sentence correctly?
☑ **2.** Did I use nouns correctly?
☑ **3.** Did I spell each word correctly?

Proofreading Marks
∧ Add
— Take out
≡ Make a capital letter
╱ Make a small letter

The Grammar/Spelling Connection

Grammar Helps
- Always name yourself last.
- The word I always is a capital letter.

Spelling Help
- The long **a** sound may be spelled a-consonant-e. (make, late)

Step 5: Publish

Todd titled his story "Jason and the Rainbow." Then he copied his story neatly. He checked it again. Todd made a storybook. Then he gave his storybook to his sister.

On Your Own

1. **Copy** Copy your story neatly. Check for mistakes.

2. **Add a title** Write a title for your story.

3. **Share** Read and show your story to your class or to someone at home.

Ideas for Sharing

- Put everyone's story title on the bulletin board. Take turns reading your stories. Match the stories and titles.
- Make a poster for your story.

Applying Story Writing

Writing Across the Curriculum
Science

Plants and animals are living things. A story about a plant or an animal would be fun to write and read. Use the five writing steps. Here are some ideas.

1. **Write an animal story.** Look at the animals in the picture. Write a story about one of them. Give your animal a name. You may want to use some words in the Word Bank.

Writing Steps

1. Choose a Topic
2. Write a First Draft
3. Revise
4. Proofread
5. Publish

Word Bank

pouch
tail
climb
striped
antlers
quills

2. **Be a tree.** Pretend that you are a young tree. Write a story about something that happens to you.

Lee enjoyed reading "Nobody." He liked stories about friends. Lee read a book about two other friends. It was called <u>George and Martha</u> by James Marshall.

Lee decided to share his book with his class. He made a stick puppet that looked like George. Then Lee pretended he was George. This is what George said about the book.

Hello, Everybody! Martha and I are hippos. We are good friends. We have five stories to tell.

I like the story about Martha's pea soup. Martha just loves pea soup. She made lots of it for me! I do not like pea soup. How could I keep from hurting Martha's feelings?

Read my book to find out what happens!

Think and Discuss
• What did you learn about the book?
• What did you learn about the characters?
• Why is this a good way to share a book?

Share Your Book

Make a Stick Puppet

1. Draw a picture of your book character on heavy paper. Color it and cut it out.

2. Paste your puppet to a flat stick. Hold the stick while you talk with your puppet.

3. Pretend you are the book character. Use the puppet to tell about the book. Talk the way you think the character would sound.

Other Activities

• Ask the puppet questions about the book. Have your puppet give the answers.

• Choose another character. Make another puppet. Have both puppets tell the story.

The Book Nook

**May I Bring a Friend?** by Beatrice De Regniers The King and Queen ask a boy to visit every day for a week.	**Night Noises and Other Mole and Troll Stories** by Tony Johnston Here are four stories about how Troll helps Mole's wishes come true.

Language and Usage
Verbs

1 Action Words

You know that every sentence has an action part. One word in the action part names the action. That word is the **verb.** What are the verbs in these sentences?

Alex runs beside the water.

She plays in the sand.

Guided Practice Tell which verb on the shell fits each sentence. Then write the verbs.

★ Boats sail .

____

1. The wind _____________.

____

2. Clams _____________ into the sand.

____

3. Fish _____________.

swim
dig
sail
blows

Summing up

▶ A **verb** names an action.

★ I make a sand house.   *make*

1. Sand fills my hair.

2. The birds fly over me.

3. The birds cry loudly.

4. I play in the sand.

5. I walk in the water.

6. My father calls me.

7. I get my pail.

8. We go home.

9. I sleep in the car.

Writing Application: A Story
Write a story about a little bird who learns to
fly. Circle the verb in each sentence.

    For Extra Practice, see p. 179.

2 | Verbs That Tell About Now

A verb can name an action that is happening now.

> One girl **swings**.
>
> Two girls **swing**.

Which naming part names one? Does the verb end with <u>s</u>?

Which naming part names more than one? Does the verb end with <u>s</u>?

Add <u>s</u> to a verb that tells about one.

Guided Practice Tell which verbs are correct.

★ Scott (slide, slides).   slides

1. Amanda and Lin (jump, jumps).
2. Two children (run, runs) for the ball.
3. A girl (tag, tags) a boy.

Now write the sentences correctly.

1. _______________________________

2. _______________________________

3. _______________________________

Summing up

▶ Add <u>s</u> to a verb that tells about one.

Independent Practice Draw a line under each correct verb. Then write the sentences.

★ The dog (chase, <u>chases</u>) its tail.

The dog chases its tail.

1. Steven and Kevin (laugh, laughs).

2. The wind (blow, blows).

3. Jerry and Rick (hold, holds) the string.

4. They (run, runs) fast.

5. The kite (rise, rises) in the air.

Writing Application: Silly Story
Write a silly story. Use these verbs somewhere in your story: freeze, boil, jump, dance, sing.

For Extra Practice, see p. 180.

3 Adding ed

Some verbs name actions that are happening now. Other verbs name actions that happened before now, or in the **past.**

> I **walk** on the beach.

> Last night I **walked** on the beach.

Add **ed** to a verb to show that something happened in the past.

Guided Practice Tell which verbs name actions that happened in the past.

★ The birds (peck, pecked) at the sand.
  pecked

1. The boats (rocked, rock) in the water.
2. The waves (wash, washed) the rocks.

Now write the sentences. Use the verbs that name actions that happened in the past.

1. ____

2. ____

Summing up

▶ Add **ed** to a verb to show that something happened in the **past.**

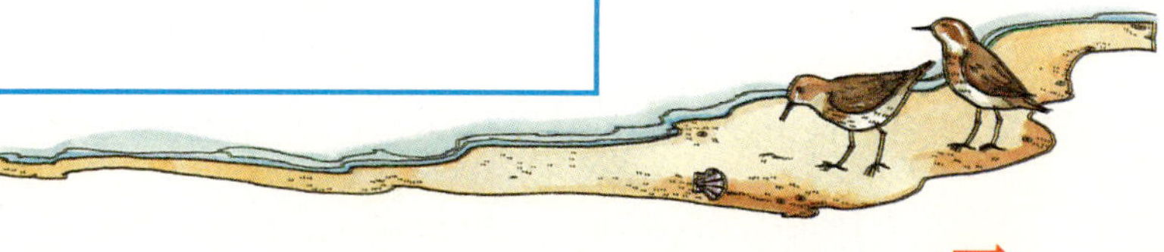

★ We (plant, <u>planted</u>) a garden.

We planted a garden.

1. We (started, start) with the corn.

2. We (finished, finish) with the beets.

3. Mary (pick, picked) plums yesterday.

4. Father (washed, wash) the plums.

5. Ben (cooked, cooks) the plums.

Writing Application: Something I Did
Write about something you did yesterday. Use
verbs that tell about the past. Circle the verbs.

For Extra Practice, see p. 181.

4 | ran, run and came, come

The **helping words** <u>have</u> and <u>has</u> are used with <u>run</u> and <u>come</u>. They are not used with <u>ran</u> and <u>came</u>. These verbs tell about the past.

Dad and Uncle Ed **came** to the race.
They **have come** often.

Uncle Ed **ran** on a team in school.
He **has run** in many races.

Guided Practice Tell the correct verbs.

★ Amy has (ran, run) to the barn. run

1. Our dog Wolf (ran, run) with her.
2. Two kittens have (ran, run) after them.
3. The kittens have (came, come) back.
4. They (came, come) back a while ago.

Now write the correct verbs.

1. ______________________

2. ______________________

3. ______________________

4. ______________________

Summing up

> ▶ <u>Have</u> and <u>has</u> are **helping words.**
> ▶ Use helping words with <u>run</u> and <u>come</u>.
> ▶ Do not use helping words with <u>ran</u> and <u>came</u>.

Independent Practice Read each
sentence. Draw a line under the correct verb.
Then write the sentence.

★ The team (<u>came</u>, come) to town.

The team came to town.

1. Brian (came, come) to the game.

2. Brian has (came, come) with me.

3. The boys (ran, run) last night.

4. They have (ran, run) a long way.

5. A dog has (ran, run) along too.

Writing Application: A Story
Write a story about two pets that ran away
from home to have an adventure and then came
back. Use the words <u>ran</u>, <u>run</u>, <u>came</u>, and <u>come</u>.

For Extra Practice, see p. 182.

5 | saw, seen and went, gone

The words <u>have</u> and <u>has</u> are used with <u>seen</u> and <u>gone</u>. They are not used with <u>saw</u> and <u>went</u>. These verbs tell about the past.

Grandpa and Jean went to the lake.

They have gone there many times.

Jean saw some frogs on the rocks.

She has seen them under rocks too.

Guided Practice Tell the correct verbs.

★ They (went, gone) along the shore.   went

1. Jean has (saw, seen) two deer there.
2. She (saw, seen) them yesterday.
3. The deer have (went, gone) away.
4. They (went, gone) into the trees.

Now write the correct verbs.

1. ____________________   3. ____________________

2. ____________________   4. ____________________

Summing up

> ▶ <u>Has</u> and <u>have</u> are helping words.
> ▶ Use helping words with <u>seen</u> and <u>gone</u>.
> ▶ Do not use helping words with <u>saw</u> and <u>went</u>.

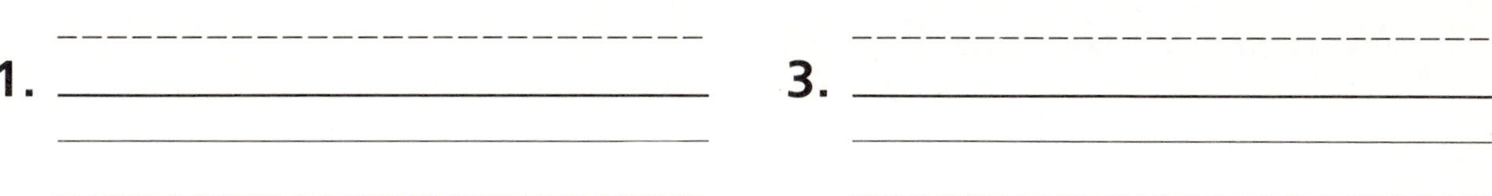

 Read each
sentence. Draw a line under the correct verb.
Then write the sentence.

★ We (<u>went</u>, gone) to the zoo.

We went to the zoo.

1. Have you (went, gone) to the zoo?

2. We (saw, seen) many animals there.

3. We have (saw, seen) the big bear.

4. Peter (went, gone) to the zoo.

5. We (saw, seen) Peter there.

Writing Application: A Story
Write a story about two friends who took a
trip. Tell where they went and what they saw.
Use the words <u>went</u>, <u>gone</u>, <u>saw</u>, and <u>seen</u>.

USAGE

6 | did, done and gave, given

The words <u>have</u> and <u>has</u> are used with <u>done</u> and <u>given</u>. They are not used with <u>did</u> and <u>gave</u>. These verbs tell about the past.

My grandmother gave us a puzzle.

She has given us many puzzles.

Matt and I did the puzzle.

We have done all of them.

Guided Practice Tell the correct verbs.

★ A clown (did, done) a funny trick.   did

1. He (did, done) the trick with balloons.
2. He has (did, done) the trick before.
3. He (gave, given) me two of the balloons.
4. I have (gave, given) one balloon away.

Now write the correct verbs.

1. _______________________

2. _______________________

3. _______________________

4. _______________________

Summing up

▶ <u>Have</u> and <u>has</u> are helping words.
▶ Use helping words with <u>done</u> and <u>given</u>.
▶ Do not use helping words with <u>did</u> and <u>gave</u>.

Independent Practice Read each
sentence. Draw a line under the correct verb.
Then write the sentence.

★ Ted has (gave, given) a report.

<u>Ted has given a report.</u>

1. Mrs. Smith (gave, given) him a good mark.

2. Julie and Pat (did, done) reports too.

3. They have (given, gave) them already.

4. They have (did, done) very well.

5. Carlos (did, done) well too.

Writing Application: A Story
Write a story about someone who was given a
prize. Tell what the person did to win it. Use
the words <u>did</u>, <u>done</u>, <u>gave</u>, and <u>given</u>.

   <u>did</u>, <u>done</u> and <u>gave</u>, <u>given</u>   For Extra Practice, see p. 184.

7 | is and are

Is and are tell about something that is happening now.

Jack **is** in the race.

Marti and Bill **are** also in the race.

Which sentence tells about one? Which sentence tells about more than one?

Use is with one. Use are with more than one.

Guided Practice Tell the correct verbs.

★ Marti and Jack (is, are) ready.   are

1. Bill (is, are) at the starting line.
2. Bill and Marti (is, are) in front.
3. They (is, are) moving fast.
4. Marti (is, are) the winner.

Now write the correct verbs.

1. __________________________

2. __________________________

3. __________________________

4. __________________________

Summing up

▶ Use is with one.
▶ Use are with more than one.

Independent Practice

A. Write <u>is</u> or <u>are</u> to finish each sentence correctly.

★ My pet _____ is _____ a rabbit.

1. Her name _____________ Fluff.

2. Her ears _____________ long.

3. Her feet _____________ black.

B. Read each sentence. Draw a line under the correct verb. Then write the sentence.

★ Becky (<u>is</u>, are) my friend.

Becky is my friend.

4. Becky and Stacy (is, are) sisters.

5. Becky (is, are) in my class.

Writing Application: Description
Write about your favorite things. Use the words <u>is</u> and <u>are</u>.

164   is and are

For Extra Practice, see p. 185.

8 | was and were

Was and were tell about something that happened in the past.

Jamie's birthday was yesterday.

The gifts were a surprise.

Which sentence tells about one? Which sentence tells about more than one?

Use was with one. Use were with more than one.

Guided Practice Tell the correct verbs.

★ The party (was, were) for Jamie. was

1. It (was, were) at Jamie's house.
2. Ten children (was, were) there.
3. The hats (was, were) red and blue.
4. Jamie (was, were) happy.

Now write the correct verbs.

1. _______________________ 3. _______________________

2. _______________________ 4. _______________________

Summing up

▶ Use was with one.
▶ Use were with more than one.

Independent Practice

A. Write <u>was</u> or <u>were</u> to finish each sentence correctly.

★ One gift __was__ from Mary.

1. Two tapes _______________ in a red box.

2. A new game _______________ from Mother.

B. Write each sentence correctly.

★ The circus (was, were) here.

The circus was here.

3. The lions (was, were) big.

4. The clown (was, were) funny.

5. His tricks (was, were) silly.

Writing Application: Description

Write about a birthday party. Use the words <u>was</u> and <u>were</u>.

For Extra Practice, see p. 186.

9 | Contractions

A **contraction** is a short way of writing words. An **apostrophe** ' shows where letters were left out.

do not	**don't**
does not	**doesn't**
is not	**isn't**
cannot	**can't**

Guided Practice Tell the contractions for these words.

★ do not   don't

1. does not

2. cannot

3. is not

Now write the contractions for the words.

1. ______________   **2.** ______________   **3.** ______________

Summing up

▶ A **contraction** is a short way of writing words.

▶ An **apostrophe** ' shows where letters have been left out.

Independent Practice

A. Write contractions for the underlined words.

★ Tim <u>does not</u> like the dark.

1. We <u>do not</u> have a fire started.

2. You <u>cannot</u> use wet wood.

3. The wood <u>is not</u> wet now.

B. Write the words that make up the contractions.

★ I <u>don't</u> go far from the tent.

4. Tim <u>doesn't</u> know his way.

5. He <u>can't</u> find the tent.

6. It <u>isn't</u> going to rain.

7. Tim <u>doesn't</u> like camping.

Writing Application: A Story

Write a story about Mr. Nobody. Use the contractions <u>don't</u>, <u>doesn't</u>, <u>can't</u>, and <u>isn't</u>.

For Extra Practice, see p. 187.

Name

Grammar-Writing Connection

Writing Clearly with Verbs

Good writers choose words that make their writing more exciting. **Verbs** are words that show action. Choosing the right verb makes a sentence come alive.

The right verb shows the action of the sentence.

Which sentence is more exciting? Which one lets you see what happened to the toy?

The toy <u>fell</u> down the stairs.

The toy <u>tumbled</u> down the stairs.

<u>Tumbled</u> tells more clearly how the toy fell.

Revising Sentences

Complete each sentence. Choose a verb that lets you see what happened.

★ The pitcher _____ hurled _____ the ball.

1. The skater _____________________ across the ice.

2. The wind _____________________ all night.

3. I _____________________ the heavy box home.

Grammar-Writing Connection

Creative Writing

Manchester Valley (1914–18?) by Joseph Pickett
The Museum of Modern Art, New York

Does this place seem still and quiet? Look again! A train is steaming along the tracks.

• What things in the picture are moving?

Activities

1. **Describe the sounds.** Write about the sounds that you would hear in this valley.

2. **Write a story.** Imagine that you are on this train. Write about your ride.

Check-up: Unit 6

Action Words (page 151)
Write the verb in each sentence.

1. A cool wind blows. _______________________

2. The leaves fall. _______________________

3. Children jump in the leaves. _______________________

Verbs That Tell About Now (page 153)
Read each sentence. Draw a line under the correct verb.

4. Jeff (play, plays) a game.

5. Brian and Andy (play, plays) too.

6. Andy (throw, throws) the ball.

7. Jeff (swings, swing) the bat.

Adding ed (page 155)
Read each sentence. Draw a line under the verb that tells about the past.

8. Last night we (watch, watched) the sky.

9. The stars (wink, winked) at us.

10. We (looked, look) for falling stars.

11. Two owls (hoot, hooted).

12. Some clouds (cover, covered) the moon.

Special Verbs (pages 157, 159, 161)

Read each sentence. Draw a line under the correct verb.

13. Jane (ran, run) home.

14. She has (came, come) from the fair.

15. Tina has (went, gone) to the fair.

16. She also (went, gone) yesterday.

17. She (saw, seen) the horses.

18. Nancy (did, done) well at the fair.

19. They (gave, given) her pony a prize.

20. I have (saw, seen) Nancy ride.

is and are (page 163)

Write is or are to finish each sentence correctly.

21. Grapes _____________ green.   **22.** A banana _____________ soft.

was and were (page 165)

Write was or were to finish each sentence correctly.

23. The bike _____________ old.   **24.** The tires _____________ flat.

Contractions (page 167)

Write the contractions for these words.

25. is not _____________   **26.** cannot _____________

Name ___________________________

Cumulative Review

The Sentence

What Is a Sentence? (pages 37–38)
Draw lines to make sentences.

1. I like   are pretty.

2. The sun   the garden.

3. The flowers   is warm.

Naming Part and Action Part
(pages 39–42)
Write a naming part or an action part in the
Word Box to finish each sentence.

made chicken soup   The soup   The children

4. ___________________________ are hungry.

5. Mother ___________________________.

6. ___________________________ tastes good.

Is It a Sentence? (pages 43–44)
Draw a line under the sentence in each pair.

7. It was a surprise.   **8.** fun to read

a letter from Jill   I answered it.

Telling Sentences and Questions (pages 45–48)
Write each sentence correctly.

9. dad took Rosa to the circus

____

____

10. did she like the monkeys

____

____

Nouns

Naming Words (pages 95–98)
Draw a line under each noun.

11. The lake was warm.   **12.** A fly buzzed.

One and More Than One (pages 99–104)
Write each noun to name more than one.

13. inch _________________   **15.** woman _________________

14. child _________________   **16.** dog _________________

Special Nouns (pages 105–106)
Write each special noun correctly.

17. I miss my friend dave. _________________

18. He moved to denver. _________________

Cumulative Review, continued

Words for Nouns (pages 107–108)

Write the pronoun in the Word Box that can take the place of the underlined word or words.

19. <u>Carlos</u> hit the ball. ________________________

20. <u>The ball</u> went far. ________________________

| He |
| They |
| It |
| She |

Naming Yourself Last (pages 109–110)

Draw a line under the correct words.

21. (James and I, I and James) made a boat.

22. (I and Ann, Ann and I) sailed in it.

Verbs

Action Words (pages 151–152)

Read each sentence. Draw a line under the verb.

23. Darlene hides.   **24.** Jason finds her.

Verbs That Tell About Now, Adding <u>ed</u>
(pages 153–156)

Read each sentence. Draw a line under the correct verb.

25. I (help, helps) clean the house.

26. Yesterday I (mow, mowed) the lawn.

Special Verbs
(pages 157–162)
Read each sentence. Draw a line under the correct verb.

27. Kim (ran, run) in the race yesterday.

28. Her family (come, came) to cheer.

29. Carla has (gone, went) to a movie.

30. I (saw, seen) her on the bus.

31. I (did, done) the jigsaw puzzle.

32. I have (gave, given) it to Cam.

is and are, was and were
(pages 163–166)
Read each sentence. Draw a line under the correct verb.

33. The show (was, were) great.

34. The clowns (is, are) very funny.

35. They (was, were) the best part.

36. One clown (is, are) my favorite.

Contractions
(pages 167–168)
Write the contractions for these words.

37. is not ______________   **39.** cannot ______________

38. do not ______________   **40.** does not ______________

Enrichment

Using Verbs

Growing Up

Fold a sheet of paper in half. Draw a picture of yourself doing something as a baby on one side. Draw a picture of yourself doing something now on the other side.

Write a sentence below each picture. Write what you are doing in each picture. Circle the verb in each sentence.

Shape Book

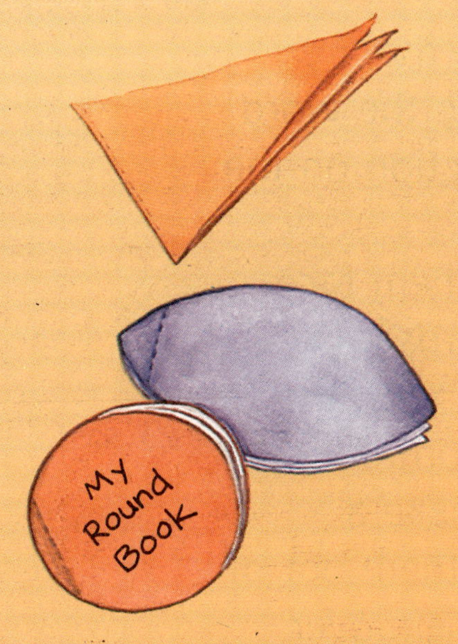

Draw and cut out a big shape, such as a circle or a square. Trace the shape two more times. Cut out the shapes. Put the shapes together to make a book.

Draw something with that shape on each page. Write a sentence about that thing.

Wave the Flag

Color a sheet of paper to look like a United States' flag. Use the colors red, white, and blue. Show the stars and the stripes.

Write two sentences about the flag on the back. Use the verbs <u>is</u> and <u>are</u>.

Contraction Match

Players   2 or more

You need   8 note cards
Use the box on page 167. Write the contractions on four cards. Write the word or words that make each contraction on the other cards.

How to play   Mix the cards. Put them face down in rows. Turn over two cards on each turn. Try to match a contraction with the word or words that make that contraction. For example, <u>cannot</u> and <u>can't</u> make a match. If the cards match, take them out of the game. If they do not, turn them over.

Scoring   The player with the most cards wins.

Extra Practice: Unit 6

1 | Action Words (page 151)

● ▲ Write the verb from the Word Box that fits in each sentence.

claps	toot	bangs	plays

★ The band **plays** music.

1. A girl _______________ the drums.

2. Two boys _______________ horns.

3. The crowd _______________ .

■ Draw a line from the Action Words Box to each action word.

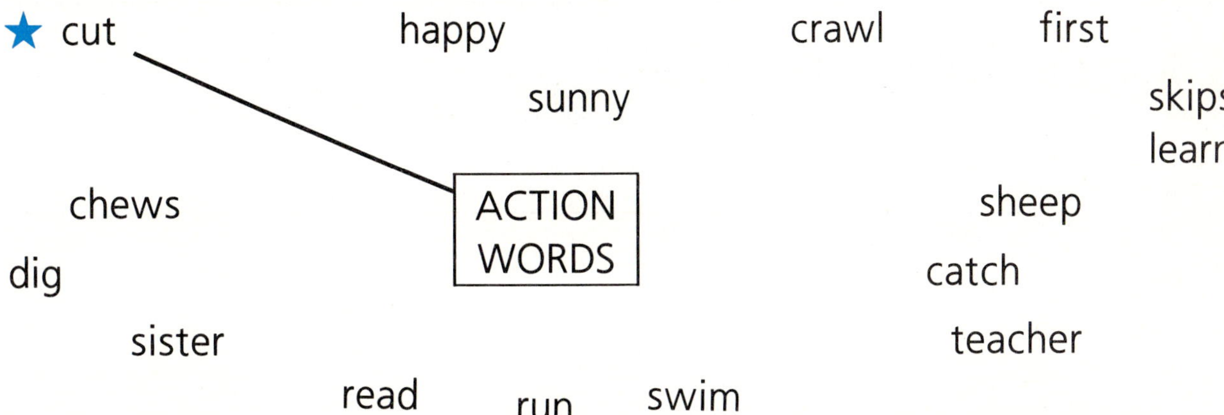

2 ‖ Verbs That Tell About Now (p. 153)

● ▲ Draw a line under each correct verb.

★ Josh (swim, <u>swims</u>).

1. Janet and Kim (talk, talks).

2. Pedro (play, plays) baseball.

3. Carol (kick, kicks) a soccer ball.

4. Doug and Dan (read, reads).

■ Write the sentences correctly.

★ Mom (make, makes) birdhouses.

Mom makes birdhouses.

5. Amy and Susie (help, helps) her.

6. Mom and Amy (cut, cuts) the wood.

7. Susie (paint, paints) the houses.

8. Amy (fill, fills) them with seeds.

3 | Adding _ed_ (p. 155)

● ▲ Draw a line under each verb that tells about the past.

★ Mother (start, <u>started</u>) the car.

1. The car (turned, turn) left.

2. We (pass, passed) the school.

3. A school bus (honked, honk) at us.

■ Rewrite each verb in ( ) so that the sentences tell about the past.

★ We _____ washed _____ the car. (wash)

4. Dad _____________________ on the water. (turn)

5. John _____________________ the bucket. (fill)

6. Ann _____________________ the windows. (spray)

7. I _____________________ them. (clean)

8. Ann _____________________ me. (splash)

9. The car _____________________ great! (look)

4 | ran, run and came, come (p. 157)

● ▲ Draw a line under the correct verb.

★ We have (came, <u>come</u>) for the party.

1. Jesse (run, ran) all the way.

2. We (came, come) an hour ago.

3. Now Joan has (run, ran) to the door.

4. Ira (came, come) with a big present.

■ Write the correct verb from the Word Box to finish each sentence.

ran	run
came	come

★ I have _________ run _________ around the playground.

5. Our parents have _________________ to the track meet.

6. The teachers _________________ a while ago.

7. Melissa _________________ in the relay race.

8. Mary _________________ too.

9. She has _________________ in every race.

5 | saw, seen and went, gone (p. 159)

● ▲ Draw a line under each correct verb.

★ Nick (<u>saw</u>, seen) many frogs at the pond.

1. He has (saw, seen) them there all summer.

2. Now summer has (went, gone).

3. Nick (went, gone) back to the pond today.

4. He (saw, seen) only a few frogs.

■ Write the correct verb from the Word Box to finish each sentence.

saw	seen	went	gone

★ Aunt Kim and I ______went______ on a whale watch.

5. Aunt Kim has __________ on one before.

6. She has __________ huge whales.

7. First, we __________ the whale's tail.

8. Then the whale __________ under the ship.

9. Now I have __________ my first whale!

6 | did, done and gave, given (page 161)

● ▲ Draw a line under each correct verb.

★ Carlos (gave, given) Rosa a book.

1. Rosa has (did, done) a report on it.

2. She has (gave, given) the report.

3. Rosa (did, done) a good job.

4. She (gave, given) the book to Sandy.

■ Write the correct verb from the Word Box in each sentence.

did	done
gave	given

★ Mary has _____given_____ the prize to David.

5. Mother _____________ apples to us.

6. Lise has _____________ a math project.

7. John has _____________ a gift to me.

8. Fran and I _____________ cartwheels.

7 | is and are (page 163)

● ▲ Draw a line under each correct verb.

★ The books (is, <u>are</u>) on my desk.

1. My pencil (are, is) lost.

2. The papers (is, are) not here.

3. Your pen (is, are) over there.

4. Our notebooks (are, is) blue.

■ Write <u>is</u> or <u>are</u> to finish each sentence correctly.

★ The zoo _______ is _______ full of animals.

5. The baby elephant _________________ wobbly.

6. It _________________ cute.

7. The lions _________________ loud.

8. The tigers _________________ striped.

9. The monkeys _________________ funny.

10. The zoo keeper _________________ near the monkeys.

8 | was and were (page 165)

● ▲ Cross out each verb that is not correct.

★ The boat ride (was, ~~were~~) on Sunday.

1. The sails (was, were) full of wind.

2. The wind (was, were) very strong.

3. White clouds (were, was) in the sky.

4. The sunshine (were, was) very bright.

■ Write the sentences correctly. Use <u>was</u> or <u>were</u>.

★ Our hike _____ fun.

Our hike was fun.

5. The climb _____ tiring.

6. The hills _____ steep.

7. The path _____ narrow.

8. We _____ very high up.

9 | Contractions (page 167)

● ▲ Write the contraction for each underlined word.

★ Dad <u>cannot</u> start the car. 

1. It <u>does not</u> have any gas. _______________

2. Now we <u>cannot</u> drive to school. _______________

3. Buses <u>do not</u> come here. _______________

4. It <u>is not</u> too far to walk. _______________

■ Write the words that make up each contraction.

★ Jimmy <u>can't</u> go to school today. 

5. His mom and dad <u>don't</u> want him to go. _______________

6. Jimmy <u>doesn't</u> feel well. _______________

7. He <u>isn't</u> getting out of bed. _______________

Literature and Writing
Instructions

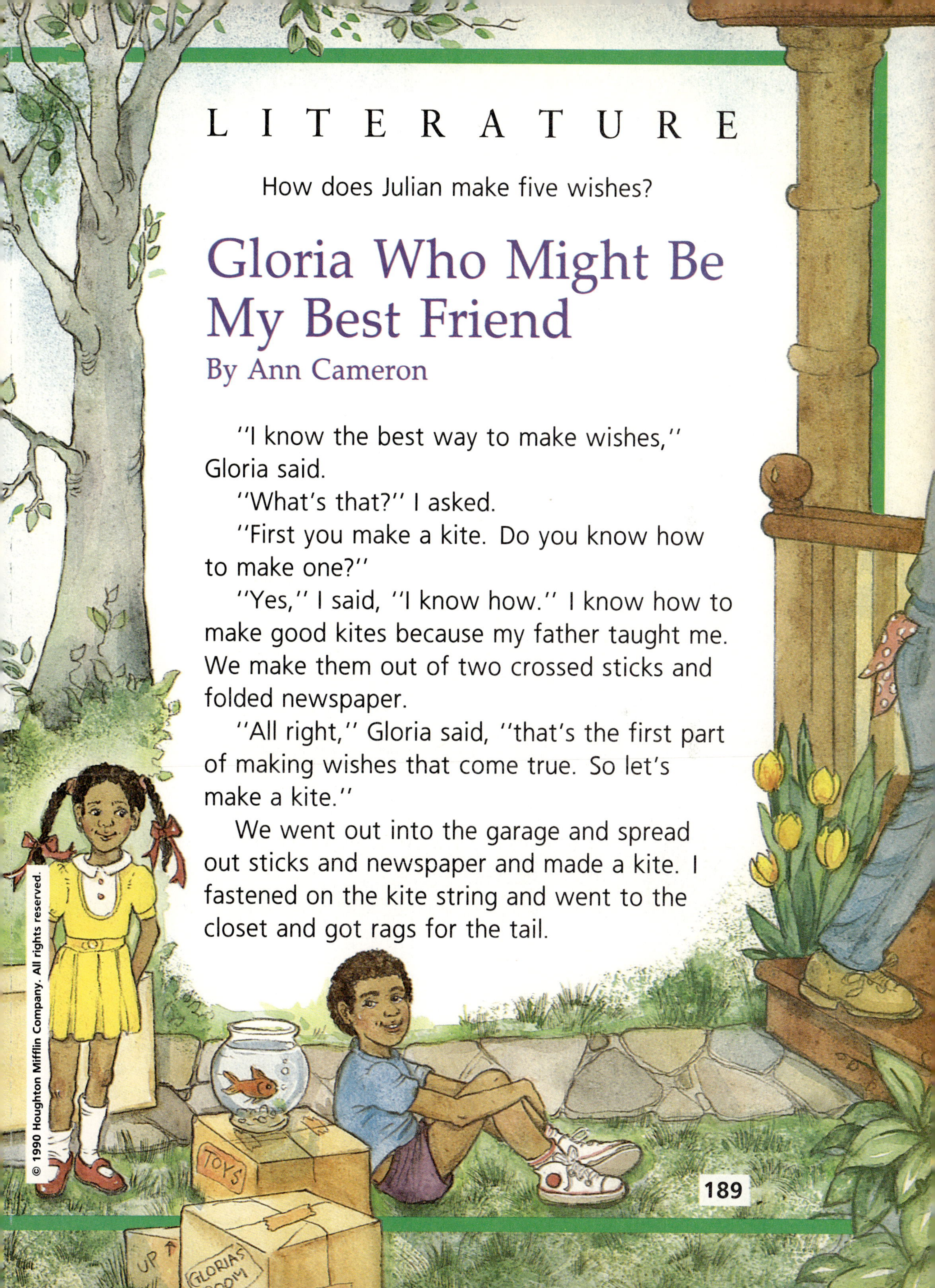

How does Julian make five wishes?

Gloria Who Might Be My Best Friend

By Ann Cameron

''I know the best way to make wishes,'' Gloria said.

''What's that?'' I asked.

''First you make a kite. Do you know how to make one?''

''Yes,'' I said, ''I know how.'' I know how to make good kites because my father taught me. We make them out of two crossed sticks and folded newspaper.

''All right,'' Gloria said, ''that's the first part of making wishes that come true. So let's make a kite.''

We went out into the garage and spread out sticks and newspaper and made a kite. I fastened on the kite string and went to the closet and got rags for the tail.

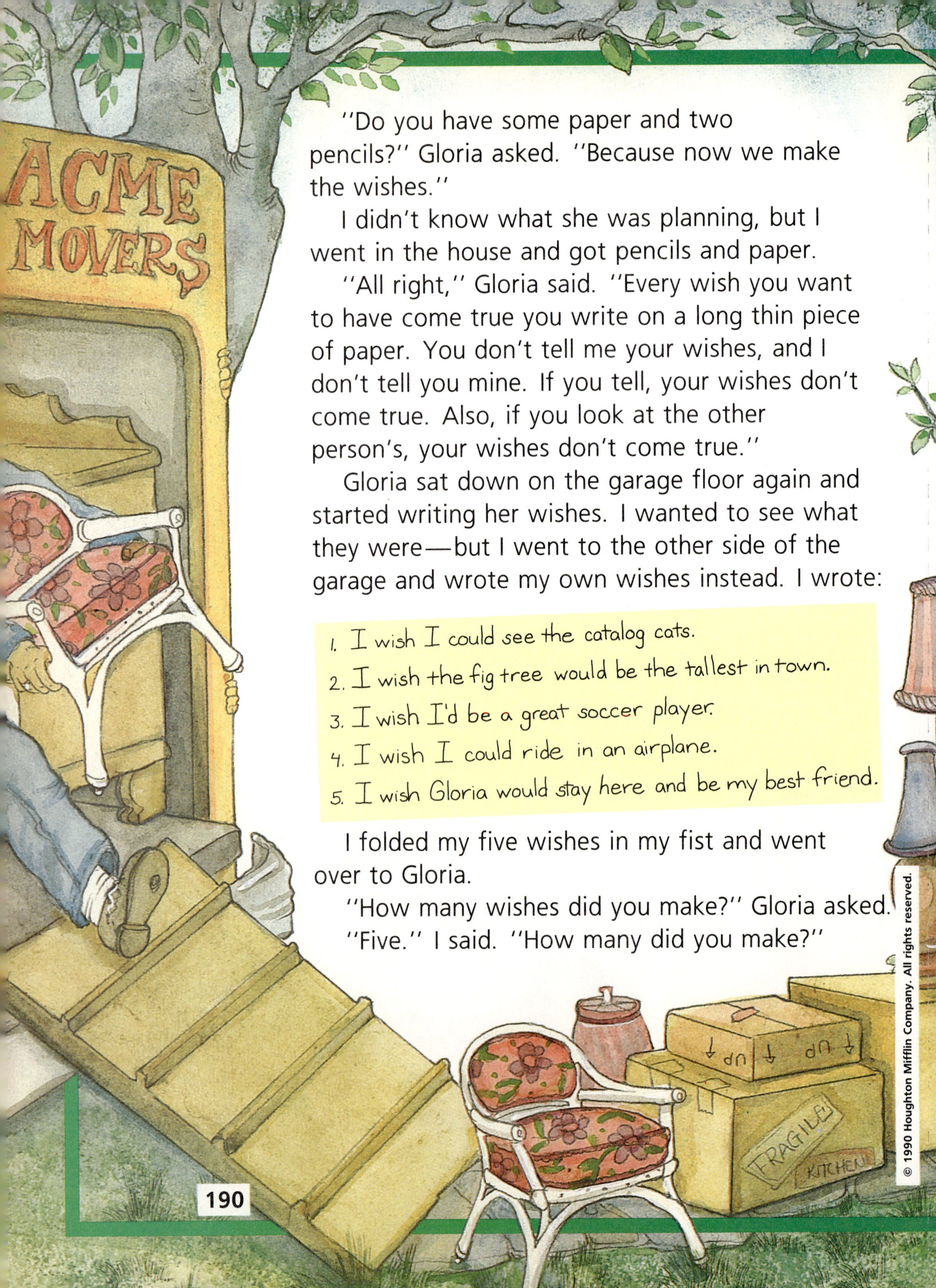

''Do you have some paper and two pencils?'' Gloria asked. ''Because now we make the wishes.''

I didn't know what she was planning, but I went in the house and got pencils and paper.

''All right,'' Gloria said. ''Every wish you want to have come true you write on a long thin piece of paper. You don't tell me your wishes, and I don't tell you mine. If you tell, your wishes don't come true. Also, if you look at the other person's, your wishes don't come true.''

Gloria sat down on the garage floor again and started writing her wishes. I wanted to see what they were—but I went to the other side of the garage and wrote my own wishes instead. I wrote:

I folded my five wishes in my fist and went over to Gloria.

''How many wishes did you make?'' Gloria asked.
''Five.'' I said. ''How many did you make?''

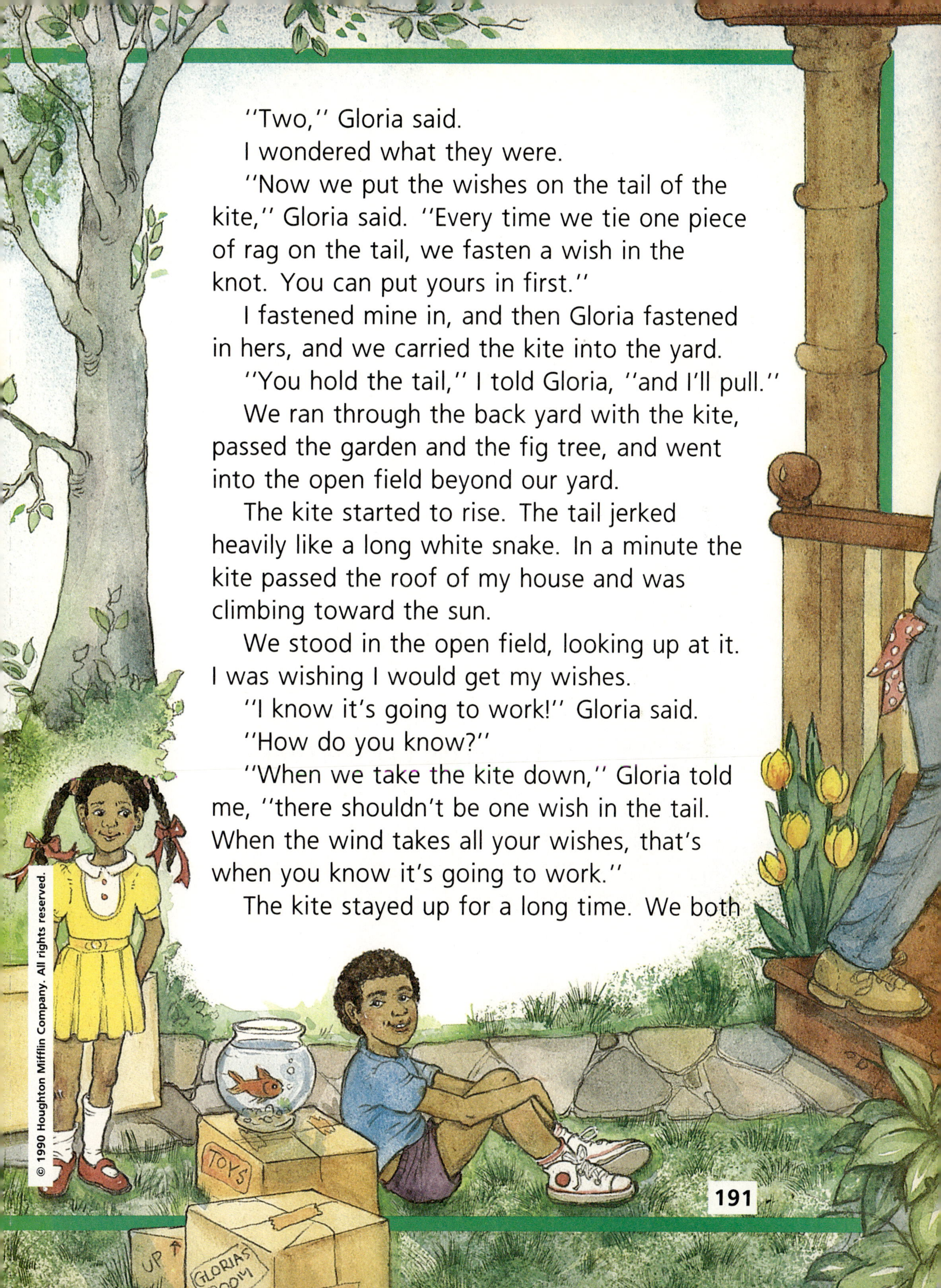

"Two," Gloria said.

I wondered what they were.

"Now we put the wishes on the tail of the kite," Gloria said. "Every time we tie one piece of rag on the tail, we fasten a wish in the knot. You can put yours in first."

I fastened mine in, and then Gloria fastened in hers, and we carried the kite into the yard.

"You hold the tail," I told Gloria, "and I'll pull."

We ran through the back yard with the kite, passed the garden and the fig tree, and went into the open field beyond our yard.

The kite started to rise. The tail jerked heavily like a long white snake. In a minute the kite passed the roof of my house and was climbing toward the sun.

We stood in the open field, looking up at it. I was wishing I would get my wishes.

"I know it's going to work!" Gloria said.

"How do you know?"

"When we take the kite down," Gloria told me, "there shouldn't be one wish in the tail. When the wind takes all your wishes, that's when you know it's going to work."

The kite stayed up for a long time. We both

held the string. The kite looked like a tiny black spot in the sun, and my neck got stiff from looking at it.

"Shall we pull it in?" I asked.

"All right," Gloria said.

We drew the string in more and more until, like a tired bird, the kite fell at our feet.

We looked at the tail. All our wishes were gone. Probably they were still flying higher and higher in the wind.

Maybe I would see the catalog cats and get to be a good soccer player and have a ride in an airplane and the tallest fig tree in town. And Gloria would be my best friend.

Think and Discuss

1. Julian wrote five wishes on a list. What did he and Gloria do with their lists then?

2. What were some of the things that Gloria and Julian did together? Do you think Gloria and Julian will become friends?

3. "Gloria Who Might Be My Best Friend" is the title of this story. Why do you think the author chose this title?

RESPONDING TO LITERATURE

The Reading and Writing Connection

Personal Response In the story, Gloria and Julian made a list of wishes. Write a wish list of your own. Which is your most important wish?

Creative Writing Think of a special way you could make a wish. Write a poem about it.

Creative Activities

Draw Your Own Kite Make a colorful kite. Cut it out. Write your wishes on strips of paper. Tape them on its tail.

Instructions for Making New Friends With a partner think up some rules for making a friend.

Vocabulary

Have you ever run like the wind? Or swum like a fish? You can describe one thing by comparing it to something else. Explain when a kite can be like

a tiny black spot   a long white   a tired
in the sun   snake   bird

VOCABULARY CONNECTION

Sound Words

Some words sound like the noises they name.

Cows **moo**.

The little bird **peeps**.

What noises might Gloria and Julian hear as they fly their kite in the open field? What makes each noise?

Practice

Look at the words in the picture. Then write the correct word to fit in each sentence.

1. The wind went ___________________.

2. Julian heard the kittens ___________________.

3. Listen to the snake ___________________.

4. Gloria heard the duck ___________________.

5. Did you hear the bee ___________________?

194

Listening: Following Instructions

Are you ready to follow instructions? Listen carefully. Listen for the order of each step. Listen to hear what comes <u>first</u>, <u>next</u>, <u>last</u>. Ask questions if you do not understand a step.

Your teacher will read Gloria's instructions about how to make wishes come true. What is the first step? What is the next important step?

Use these helps when you are listening to instructions.

Listening Helps

1. Listen to all the steps.
2. Listen for order words. Some order words are <u>first</u>, <u>next</u>, <u>last</u>.
3. Ask questions if you do not understand.

Practice

Listen as your teacher reads some instructions. Follow each step to finish drawing the kite.

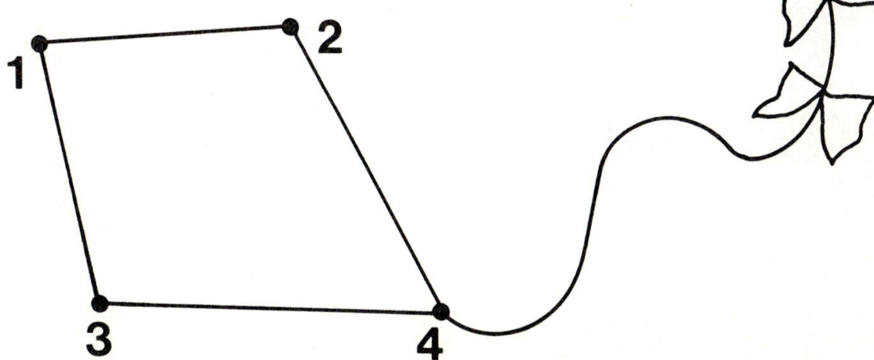

Speaking: Giving Instructions ☑

Do you remember where Gloria and Julian flew their kite? They ran through the backyard. They ran past the garden. They passed the fig tree. Finally they ran to the open field.

Pretend Gloria's mother wanted to find Gloria. What instructions might you give her? Try using words like <u>turn right</u> or <u>turn left</u>. They help make your instructions clearer.

Use these helps when you give instructions.

Speaking Helps

1. Think about the order of each step.
2. Give the steps in order from first to last.
3. Use order words to tell when to do each step.
4. Use words such as <u>right</u> and <u>left</u> when you give instructions for going to a place.

Practice

Find a partner. Take turns giving each other instructions for going to different rooms of your school. Are your instructions clear?

Thinking: Sequencing ☑

Can you put these steps in order?

Finally, go fly your kite.

Next, make the body of the kite.

Then fasten the kite tail on.

First, get newspaper and sticks.

Is it easy to put these steps in order? It is if you think about <u>how</u> to make a kite. You think about the order that makes the most sense.

Ask yourself these questions when putting steps in order.

Thinking Helps

1. What do I know about the instructions?
2. What order makes the most sense?
3. Where can I use order words such as <u>first</u>, <u>next</u>, and <u>finally</u> to help make the order clear?

Practice

A. These instructions are out of order. Number
the steps in the right order.

_____ Play some games.   _____ Next, invite the friend to play.

_____ First, phone a friend.   _____ Thank your friend for coming.

_____ Finally, wave good-by.

B. Read the instructions for making puppets
below. Then write them in order. Start
each sentence with an order word. Use the
order words in the box.

Then	First,	Next,	Finally,

Sew the buttons on the socks for eyes. Give a
puppet show for your friends. Get some old
socks, buttons, thread, and yarn. Glue the yarn
on for hair.

What Is a Paragraph? ☑

A **paragraph** is a group of sentences. All the sentences in a paragraph tell about one main idea.

A paragraph is **indented.** This means that there is a space before the first word.

What is the main idea of the paragraph below?

> Here is what you should do if you discover a bird's nest. Look at it carefully, but do not get too close. Do not make any noise. Look at how the nest is made. If you see some eggs, notice their color and shape. Never touch an egg.

The main idea is <u>what you should you do if you discover a bird's nest.</u>

Which line is indented? How do you know?

Prewriting Practice

A. Copy this paragraph. Remember to indent.

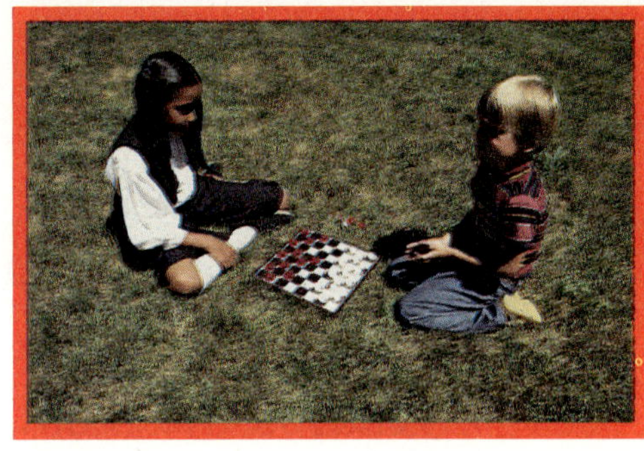

   Friends are special people. They like to play the same games as you. They understand your jokes. They know when you are happy or sad without your saying.

B. Which sentence below tells the main idea of the paragraph? Write that sentence.

1. Friends know when you are happy or sad.

2. Friends are special people.

COMPOSITION SKILL

What Is a Topic Sentence? ☑

You know that all the sentences in a paragraph tell about one main idea. Often one sentence in the paragraph tells that main idea. This sentence is called the **topic sentence.**

Read this paragraph. What is the main idea? Which sentence tells the main idea?

> There are three things to do to make a wish. Think about what you want most. Next, practice saying your wish to yourself. Then wait for the perfect time to make your wish. Maybe it will come true!

The main idea is <u>there are three things to do to make a wish</u>. Why is the first sentence the topic sentence?

Prewriting Practice

A. Find the topic sentence in this paragraph.
Write the topic sentence.

Here's what to do to make friends.
Don't laugh if they can't do a good
cartwheel. Ask them if they want to
see your tree fort. Let them know that
you think they are special.

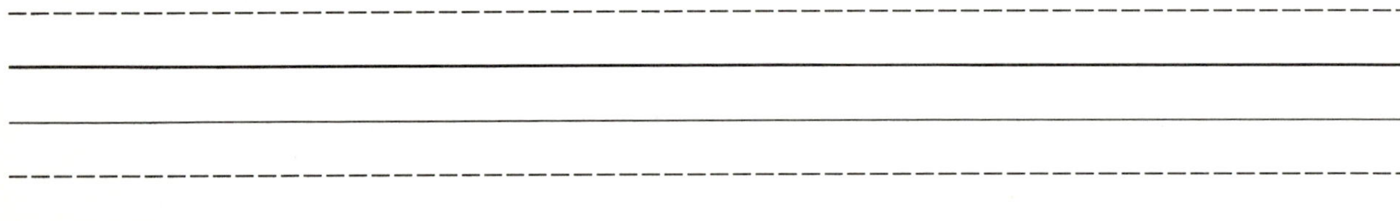

B. Read this paragraph. What is a good topic
sentence for this paragraph?

Alice and I always play together.
We like the same songs. We like the
same books. We even like the same
vegetable—spinach. I can't think of a
better friend.

Write a topic sentence for the paragraph.

Step 1: Prewriting—Choose a Topic

Anne thought of all the things she knew how to do well. She listed as many ideas as she could think of. Then she asked herself which idea would make the best instructions.

how to tie a shoe

Anne wasn't sure if she could explain all the steps clearly.

how to fold a paper hat

She wasn't sure if she could remember exactly how to make a paper hat.

how to make place mats

Anne had just made place mats using leaves and flowers. She knew all the steps, and she could explain them clearly. This was her best idea. Anne circled how to make place mats.

On Your Own

1. **Think** Think about something you can do well. Use the Ideas page to help you. Make a list of ideas.

2. **Choose** Which idea would make the best instructions? Ask yourself these questions about each of your ideas.

   Do I want to write about this idea?
   Do I know all the steps?
   Can I explain each step clearly?

   Circle a topic from your list. Then finish this sentence.

   I want to write instructions about ______________________

3. **Try it** What will your instructions be about? Do an activity under "Thinking About Your Topic" on the Ideas page.

204   The Writing Process

Ideas for Getting Started

Choosing Your Topic

Topic Ideas

how to plant a flower   how to brush your teeth
how to make breakfast   how to make paper chains

Getting Started

Ask yourself these questions. They may give you some ideas.

What do I like to do?   What do I like to make?

Thinking About Your Topic

Step-by-Step Notes

Write a few words about each step of your instructions on a sheet of paper. Draw a picture to go with each step. Here are Anne's step-by-step notes.

Talk About It

Show a friend your notes. Do you need to add any steps?

Step 2: Write a First Draft

Anne thought about all the steps for her instructions. She thought about the order. Then she wrote her first draft. She did not worry about making mistakes.

Anne's first draft

Here's a ~~good~~ fun way to make place mats. First, get two peses of wax paper. next, go outside and find some leaves and flowers. Come inside and arrange the leaves and flowers on one pese of wax paper. Finally, ask a grown-up to help you iron the two peses of wax paper together Now set the table with your new mats.

Think and Discuss

- Could you follow Anne's instructions?
- Did she leave out any steps?

On Your Own

1. **Ask yourself** Think about what you want to write. Answer these questions.

> Can I name all the steps?
> Are the steps in the right order?
> Can I use order words like <u>first</u>, <u>next</u>,
>   <u>then</u>, and <u>finally</u>?
> Can I explain each step clearly?

2. **Write** Be sure that your instructions are clear. Do not worry about making mistakes. You can make changes later.

Step 3: Revise

Anne read her instructions to herself. She added an order word. Anne asked Nadia to listen to her instructions.

Nadia liked Anne's idea for place mats. She thought there was a step missing, too. She also thought there was a step that was unclear.

Reading and responding

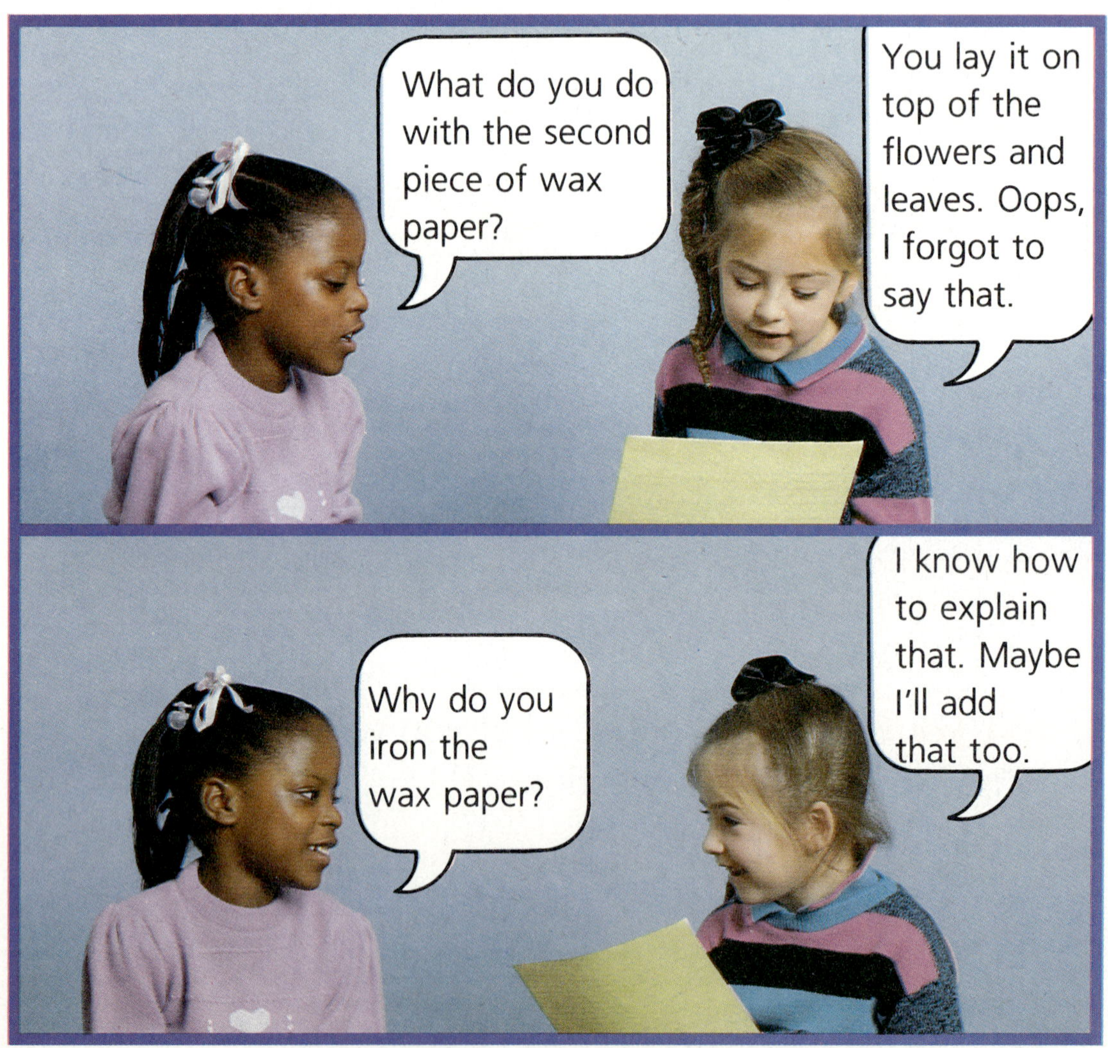

Anne added new ideas to her instructions. The new ideas helped make her writing clearer. Read Anne's revised story on the next page.

Anne's revised instructions

Here's a ~~good~~ fun way to make place mats. First, get two peses of wax paper. next, go outside and find some leaves and flowers. Then Come inside and arrange the leaves and flowers on one pese of wax paper. Put the other sheet of paper on top. Finally, ask a grown-up to help you iron the two peses of wax paper together. Now set the table with your new mats.

This will melt the wax and hold the papers together.

Think and Discuss ☑

- What order word did Anne add?
- What other changes did Anne make? Why?

On Your Own

Revising checklist

- ☑ Did I tell about one main idea?
- ☑ Do I have a topic sentence?
- ☑ Are all my steps in order?

1. **Revise** Add any steps that you forgot. Add ideas that help explain your instructions. Cross out steps that do not belong in your instructions.

2. **Have a conference** Read your instructions to a classmate. Talk about how to make your instructions clearer.

210 **The Writing Process** **See the Thesaurus on page 347.**

Step 4: Proofread

Anne was ready to proofread her story. She checked for capitals and end marks. She used the dictionary to check her spelling.

Part of Anne's proofread instructions

Here's a ~~good~~ fun way to make place mats. First, get two pieces of wax paper. next, go outside and find some leaves and flowers. Then Come inside and arrange the leaves and flowers on one piece of wax paper. Put the other sheet of paper on top. Finally, ask a grown-up to help you iron the two pieces of wax paper together. Now set the table with your new mats.

Think and Discuss

- Which word was not spelled correctly?
- Where did Anne add a capital letter and a period? Why?
- What other corrections did she make?

1. **Proofreading Practice** There are two mistakes in each sentence. Write each sentence correctly.

a. Do you kno how to bathe a dog.

b. first, change into old clothes

c. Then you finds a tub?

d. the tub should have no holees.

e. Do'nt forget sope and water.

f. Next, Scrub until your dog are clean.

g. Finally, dri your happe dog!

2. Proofread Proofread your instructions. Use
the checklist and proofreading marks to help.

<table>
<tr><td>

Proofreading Checklist

☑ **1.** Did I begin and end each
sentence correctly?

☑ **2.** Did I use verbs correctly?

☑ **3.** Did I spell each word correctly?

</td><td>

Proofreading Marks

∧ Add

— Take out

≡ Make a capital letter

/ Make a small letter

</td></tr>
</table>

The Grammar/Spelling Connection

Grammar Helps

Remember these rules for using verbs.

- Add <u>s</u> to a verb that tells about one.
- Add <u>ed</u> to a verb to show that something happened in the past.
- Use <u>is</u> with one. Use <u>are</u> with more than one.

Spelling Helps

- The long **e** sound may be spelled <u>ee</u> or <u>ea</u>. (<u>seem</u>, <u>clean</u>)
- The long **e** sound at the end of a word may be spelled <u>y</u>. (<u>happy</u>, <u>many</u>)

Step 5: Publish

Anne wrote a title for her instructions. Then she copied her paper neatly and checked it. Anne made a place mat at home and taped her instructions to it for her class to see.

On Your Own

1. **Copy** Copy your instructions neatly. Check your paper for mistakes.

2. **Add a title** Write a title for your instructions.

3. **Share** Show your instructions to your class or to someone at home.

Idea for Sharing

Draw each step of your instructions on a piece of paper. Mix up the pictures so that they are not in order. Give a classmate your instructions and your pictures. See if your classmate can put your pictures in order.

Writing Across the Curriculum
Social Studies

A <u>community</u> is a group of people. They work and play together. People in a community help each other. What instructions could you write that would help others in your community? Here are some ideas. Use the five writing steps.

1. **Tell how to help.** How are people helping in these pictures? What instructions might you give to the children in one of these pictures? Write your instructions. You may find the words in the Word Bank helpful.

Writing Steps

1. Choose a Topic
2. Write a First Draft
3. Revise
4. Proofread
5. Publish

Word Bank

together
working
jobs
cleaning
helping

2. **Explain your job.** Do you have jobs at school or at home? Write instructions that tell how to do one of your jobs.

Jessie read ''Gloria Who Might Be My Best Friend.'' Next, she read the other stories in the same book. The book is called <u>The Stories Julian Tells</u> by Ann Cameron. Jessie wanted her classmates to know about this book. She made this book jacket.

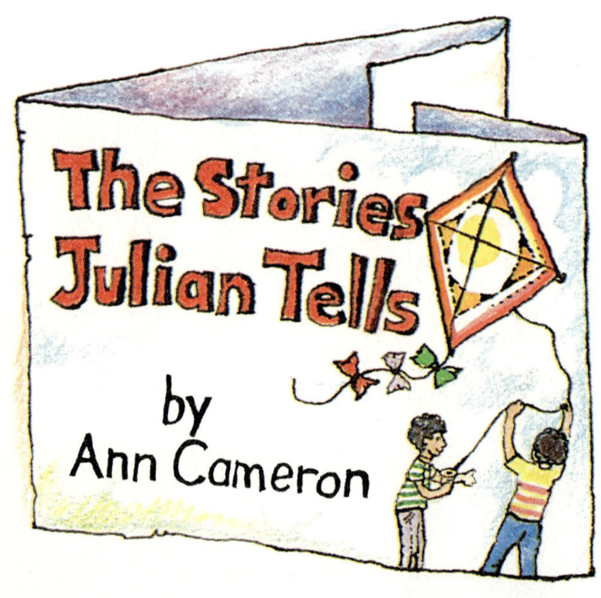

Think and Discuss

- What characters does Jessie tell about?
- What happens in the book?
- Which sentence makes you wonder what else happens in the book?

Share Your Book

Make a Book Jacket

1. Put your book on a large piece of paper. Cut and fold the paper to fit your book.
2. Draw a picture on the front cover. Then write the title and author.
3. On the back cover, write about the most exciting parts. Do not tell the whole story.

Other Activities

- Show the outside of your book jacket. Read aloud what you have written.
- Pretend that you are the main character in your book. Write about one thing that happens to you.

 **The Book Nook** 

More Stories Julian Tells by Ann Cameron	**Through Grandpa's Eyes** by Patricia MacLachlan
Julian tells more stories about Huey, Gloria, and himself.	John learns the way his blind grandpa sees the world.

Language and Usage
Adjectives

1 | How Something Looks

A word that tells how something looks is an **adjective.** Adjectives can tell size, shape, color, and how many.

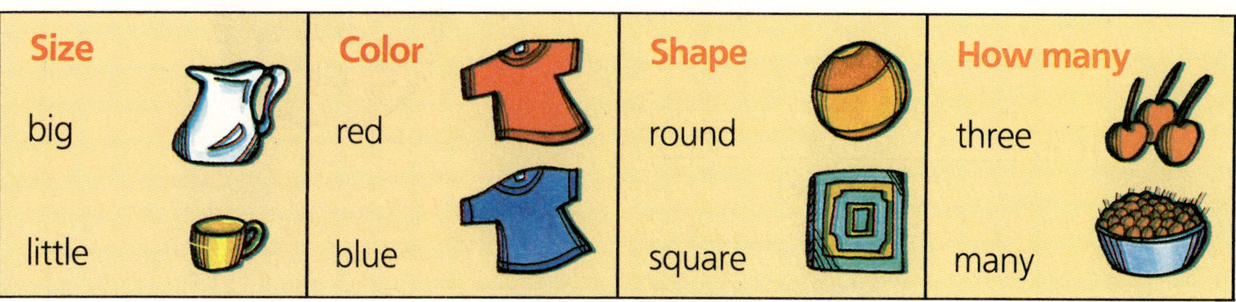

Guided Practice Tell the adjective from the Word Box that best fits each sentence. Then write the adjectives.

★ Ben has _____**three**_____ kittens.
(how many)

____

1. He likes the _____________ one best.
(color)

____

2. Button is still very _____________.
(size)

____

3. Button has a _____________ face.
(shape)

| orange |
| small |
| round |
| three |

Summing up

▶ **Adjectives** tell how something looks.

Independent Practice

A. Pick words from the berry. Write an adjective for each sentence.

★ The berry is <u>blue</u>.
(color)

1. It is ______________.
(shape)

2. The berry is very ______________.
(size)

B. Write the adjectives in each sentence.

★ This bug is red and black.

<u>red</u>   <u>black</u>

3. This bug is long and spotted.

______________   ______________

4. This bug is tall and green.

______________   ______________

Writing Application: Creative Writing

Write a poem about a butterfly. Use many adjectives in the poem. Try to make the lines rhyme. Circle all the adjectives.

For Extra Practice, see p. 232.

2 | How Something Tastes and Smells

Adjectives tell how something looks. They also tell how something tastes and smells.

Guided Practice Tell the adjective from the Word Box that best fits each sentence. Then write the adjectives.

★ This toothpaste tastes <u>minty</u>.

1. The stew smells __________.

2. The lemon tastes __________.

3. The corn tastes __________.

| salty |
| minty |
| sour |
| spicy |

Summing up

▶ Adjectives tell how something tastes and smells.

Independent Practice

A. Write the adjective from the Word Box that best fits each sentence.

★ The flowers smell .

1. The boat smells ___________.

2. The toast tastes ___________.

burnt
fishy
sweet

B. Write the word that describes the underlined word in each sentence.

★ The <u>forest</u> smells piney. 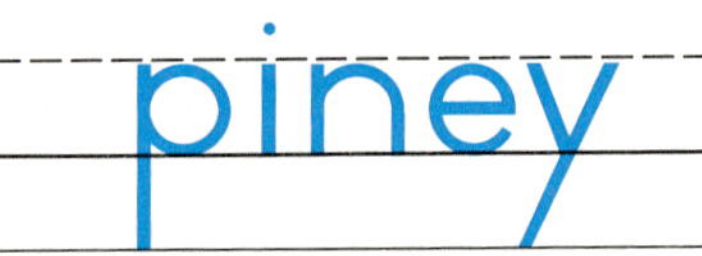

3. The <u>grapes</u> taste ripe. ___________

4. The <u>peach</u> tastes sweet. ___________

5. The <u>carrot</u> tastes bitter. ___________

6. The <u>fire</u> smells smoky. ___________

Writing Application: **Description**
Write about a food you like. Write about how it tastes and smells.

For Extra Practice, see p. 233.

3 | How Something Sounds and Feels

Adjectives tell how something looks, tastes, and smells. Adjectives also tell how something sounds and feels.

Guided Practice Tell the adjective from the Word Box that best fits each sentence. Then write the adjectives.

★ Duffy gave a _loud_ bark.

1. The car horn made a _honking_ sound.

2. Duffy licked Lenny's _smooth_ hand.

3. Lenny patted Duffy's _shaggy_ coat.

shaggy
smooth
~~loud~~
honking

Summing up

▶ Adjectives tell how something sounds and feels.

Independent Practice Use a word from
the Word Box to complete each sentence.
Write the sentences.

furry	happy
cold	heavy
splashing	

★ The rain feels ____.

The rain feels cold.

1. Anita has a ____ hat.

Anita has a furry

2. We heard a ____ laugh.

3. Who is carrying a ____ bag?

4. My boots make a ____ sound.

Writing Application: An Animal I Know
Think of an animal. Write about how it sounds
and how it feels to touch. Read what you
wrote. Can the class guess your animal?

For Extra Practice, see p. 234.

4 | Adding er and est

Adjectives can tell how things are different from each other. Add <u>er</u> to adjectives to compare two people or things. Add <u>est</u> to compare more than two people or things.

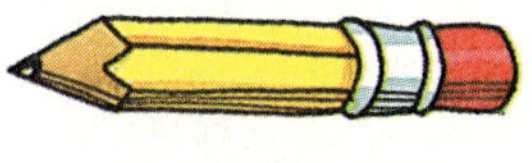

long

long**er**

long**est**

Guided Practice Tell the correct word for each sentence. Then write the words.

★ Cam is (taller, tallest) than Beth.
　taller

1. Beth is (taller, tallest) than Sue. ______________________

2. Cam is the (taller, tallest) of the three girls. ______________________

3. Mike is (shorter, shortest) than Ben. ______________________

4. Mike is the (shorter, shortest) boy in the class. ______________________

Summing up

▶ Add <u>er</u> to compare two people or things.
▶ Add <u>est</u> to compare more than two people or things.

Independent Practice Write the correct
word for each sentence.

★ A duck is (smaller, smallest)
than a turkey.

smaller

1. A horse is (faster, fastest)
than a dog.

2. The cat has (shorter, shortest)
ears than a rabbit.

3. A rabbit jumps (higher, highest)
than a mouse.

4. The turtle is the (slower,
slowest) of all these animals.

5. Which of the animals is the
(faster, fastest) of them all?

Writing Application: A Story
Write a story about a pet dog that became
smaller and smaller until it was the smallest
dog in the world. What kinds of problems
would it have?

For Extra Practice, see p. 235.

Grammar-Writing Connection

Writing Clearly with Adjectives

Writers use **adjectives** to add special details to sentences. They can tell how something looks, tastes, smells, sounds, and feels.

Which sentence tells you more?

The horn sounds like a cow.

The rusty, old horn sounds like a tired cow.

The second sentence tells us the horn is old and rusty and the cow is tired.

Revising Sentences

Complete each sentence with an adjective that adds more detail.

★ The _______ black _______ dog barked.

1. I jumped over the _______________ fence.

2. The _______________ children ran home.

3. We lost our _______________ frog.

4. Look at the _______________ cat.

Grammar-Writing Connection

Creative Writing

Illustration by
N. C. Wyeth

Do you have a pet that you love? This picture shows the love between a boy and a pet deer.

- Why does this picture seem warm and cozy?

Activities

1. **Write a story.** How did the boy find the deer? Write a story about them.
2. **Describe your pet.** Tell what kind of pet you would like and why you would choose it.

Enrichment

Using Adjectives

Riddle Pictures

Make riddle pictures. Use three sheets of paper. Write a riddle on one side. Use three describing words. Draw a picture of the answer on the back. Trade riddles with a classmate. Guess the answers to your classmate's riddles.

Clowning Around

Make a clown face with describing words. First, draw and cut out a large circle from a sheet of paper. Draw and cut out the eyes, ears, nose, and mouth. Write a describing word that tells how something tastes on the mouth. Write sight words on the eyes, sound words on the ears, and a smell word on the nose. Paste them on the clown face. Add hair and a hat.

Extra Practice: Unit 8

1 | How Something Looks (page 219)

● ▲ Write the adjective from the Word Box that best fits each sentence.

★ The store sold ___**one**___ beach ball.
(how many)

1. The beach balls are _______________.
(shape)

2. This one is very _______________.
(size)

3. It has big _______________ dots.
(color)

large
round
green
one

■ Find the adjectives. Draw a line under each one.

★ The toys are <u>small</u>. (size)

4. The car is red. (color)

5. A thin stripe is down its side. (size)

6. The tires are wide. (size)

7. I have six cars. (how many)

8. I like the blue car best. (color)

9. It has four doors. (how many)

2 How Something Tastes and Smells (page 221)

●▲ Write the adjective from the Word Box that best fits each sentence.

ripe	spicy
stale	smoky

★ The banana smells __ripe__.

1. The old crackers taste ________.

2. Our campfire smells ________.

3. Many Mexican foods taste ________.

■ Draw a line under the word that describes the underlined word in each sentence.

★ The <u>stew</u> tastes <u>peppery</u>.

4. The <u>wash</u> smells soapy.

5. The <u>milk</u> tastes sour.

6. The <u>woods</u> smell piney.

7. The <u>rose</u> smells sweet.

3 | How Things Sound and Feel(p. 223)

● ▲ Write the adjective from the Word Box that best fits in each sentence.

cool   hot   loud   soft

★ The sun feels 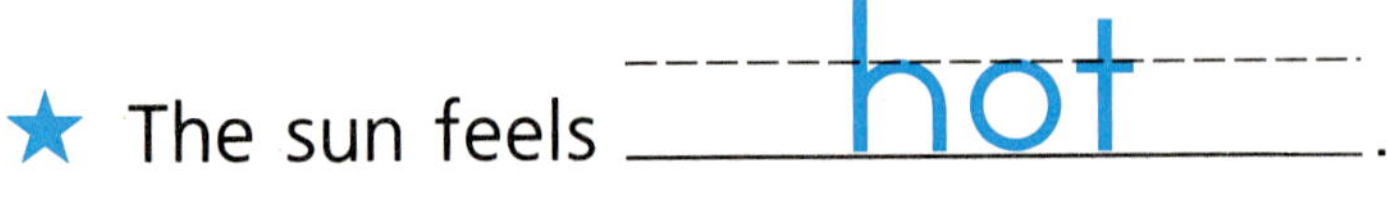.

1. A whisper sounds _____________.

2. The shade feels _____________.

3. The horn sounds _____________.

■ Finish each sentence. Use a verb and the adjective in the box.

wet

★ The snow 

slippery

4. The street _____________________

silent

5. The flakes of snow _____________

4 | Adding <u>er</u> and <u>est</u> (p. 225)

● ▲ Draw a line under the correct word.

★ Is my room (smallest, <u>smaller</u>) than yours?

1. The bookcase is (taller, tallest) than the door.

2. This is the (stronger, strongest) of all the chairs.

3. Which of these four rooms is (smaller, smallest)?

4. The wall is (cleanest, cleaner) than the floor.

■ Add <u>er</u> or <u>est</u> to the adjective.
Write the sentence correctly.

★ Jim is (short) than Sue.

<u>Jim is shorter than Sue.</u>

5. Sue is the (old) of three children.

6. Lee is (young) than Tom.

The bar is smooth
beneath our knees.
Our hands are strong,
we sit at ease.

Zilpha Keatley Snyder
from ''Spinning Song''

What do two children see, hear, and feel when they get up early one morning?

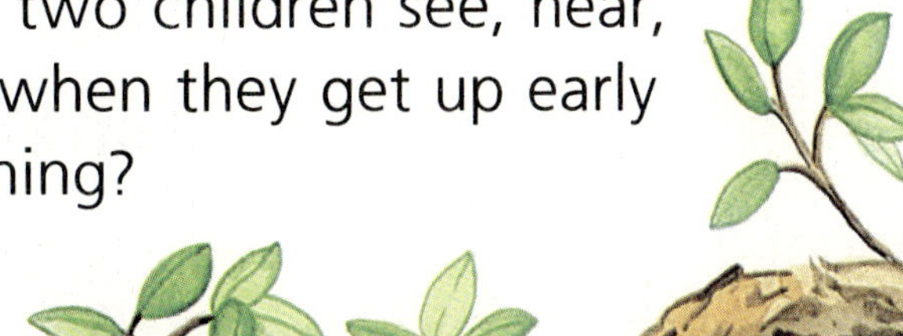

The Day We Saw the Sun Come Up

By Alice E. Goudey

One summer morning,
very, very early,
before our mother was up,
before our father was up,
before the sun was up,
my sister, Sue, and I
got up and dressed
and went outdoors.

We'd never,
in all our lives,
been up so early in the morning.
The world was very still.

It seemed as if someone
had said,
"Hush! Go quietly!
The world is not awake."
The grass was wet with dew,
and all about,
spread out on the grass,
were lacy spider webs.

We saw our cat, Christopher,
coming out across the yard,
stepping high,
and stopping to shake the dew
from each front paw
before he took another step.

We saw
the eastern sky
above the hill
all streaked with pearly pink
just like the inside of a scallop shell.
It looked as if,
hidden behind the hill,
some great light
was glowing there.
We stood still
and watched the light grow brighter.

And then,
we saw
what we had never seen before—
a small, bright edge of sun
come up above the hill.
Without a sound,
the golden sun
was rising.
After its first bright edge
peeped up above the hill,
it kept on rising
until, at last,
we saw the whole big, round sun
hanging in the eastern sky
like a great ball
made of fire.

Think and Discuss

1. What are some of the things the two
   children saw and heard early one morning?
   How do you think the children felt?

2. Why was the cat stepping high?

3. The **setting** tells where and when a story
   takes place. Where does this story take
   place? When does it take place?

What are the three main kinds of clouds? How
are they different from one another?

Clouds

By Tomie de Paola

Clouds are little drops of water or ice
hanging in the upper atmosphere high above
the earth. . . .

There are many different kinds of clouds.
Some are high up, some are in the middle, and
some are low down in the sky. The three main
kinds are called <u>cirrus</u>, <u>cumulus</u>, and <u>stratus</u>
clouds. You can tell them apart by the way
they look and by where they are in the sky.

<u>Cirrus</u> clouds are white and feathery and
they are the highest clouds. They are
sometimes called "mares' tails."

<u>Cumulus</u> clouds are puffy and look like
cauliflowers. They also have flat bottoms. They
are always changing shape and are low down
in the sky.

240

Stratus clouds are low also. They look like
wide blankets of gray and are sometimes called
"high fogs." Drizzle or snow flurries may fall
from them.

There are some sayings about clouds that
help tell about the weather.

"Evening red and morning gray
Set the traveler on his way.

Evening gray and morning red
Bring down rain upon his head."

Think and Discuss

1. What are clouds made of? Name the three
   main kinds of clouds. How are they
   different from one another?

2. Read the last four lines of "Clouds" again.
   What does this saying tell about the
   weather? How do you think this saying
   came to be?

3. "Clouds" is **nonfiction.** It tells about things
   that are true, not make-believe. How are
   "Clouds" and "The Day We Saw the Sun
   Come Up" different?

Can you figure out
what this poem is about?

White sheep, white sheep,
  On a blue hill,
When the wind stops,
  You all stand still.

When the wind blows,
  You walk away slow.
White sheep, white sheep,
  Where do you go?

(Author unknown)

Think and Discuss

1. What are the "white sheep" in this poem? What is the "blue hill"? What is a good title for this poem?

2. What happens when the wind stops? What happens when the wind blows?

3. In poems, we say certain words or parts of words louder than others. Saying it louder is called **stress.** Read the poem quietly to yourself. Try to say these words a little louder than the rest: <u>white</u>, <u>white</u>, <u>hill</u>, <u>stops</u>, <u>still</u>, <u>blows</u>, <u>slow</u>, <u>white</u>, <u>white</u>, <u>go</u>.

RESPONDING TO LITERATURE

The Reading and Writing Connection

Personal Response Which one of these reading selections did you like best? Write some sentences telling why you chose the one you did.

Creative Writing Pretend that you are riding on a cloud. Where does it take you? What do you see and feel? Write a story that tells about your ride.

Creative Activities

Read Aloud With your class, read aloud ''The Day We Saw the Sun Come Up.'' What do you think the writer saw and heard <u>after</u> the sun came up? Take turns adding lines to the end of the story.

Draw Imagine watching the sun come up. What would it look like? What colors would it be? Draw and color your own sunrise.

Vocabulary

A mare is a female horse. What is a colt? What is a foal? Look up <u>colt</u> and <u>foal</u> in a dictionary.

VOCABULARY CONNECTION

Getting the Meaning

Sometimes the words in a sentence can help you decide the meaning of a new word.

> Clouds are little drops of water or ice hanging in the upper <u>atmosphere</u> high above the earth.
>
> from "Clouds" by Tomie de Paola

Which words help you decide the meaning of <u>atmosphere</u>? Which word in the cloud gives the meaning of <u>atmosphere</u>?

Practice

Read the sentences. Write the word in the Word Box that gives the meaning of the underlined word from "Clouds."

rain	horse	snowfall

★ The <u>mare</u> galloped across the field.   horse

1. The light <u>drizzle</u> wet my hair.
2. The <u>flurries</u> made the ground white.

1. _______________________   2. _______________________

244

Listening for Details ☑

Words can paint pictures in your mind. Listen as your teacher reads to you from "The Day We Saw the Sun Come Up." What picture can you see?

What did the sun look like just as it was beginning to rise? What did it sound like?

The words <u>small</u>, <u>bright</u>, and <u>edge of sun</u> tell what the sun looked like as it started to rise. The words <u>without a sound</u> tell what it sounded like.

These words are **details** from the story. The **details** give a clear picture of the rising sun.

Listen carefully for details. They can paint a picture in your mind.

Listening Help

Listen for words that tell what something is like.

Practice

Listen as your teacher reads to you. Remember the Listening Help. Then draw a picture. Show the details you heard.

Thinking: Observing ☑

Think about the story ''The Day We Saw the Sun Come Up.'' What could the two children see, hear, smell, and feel?

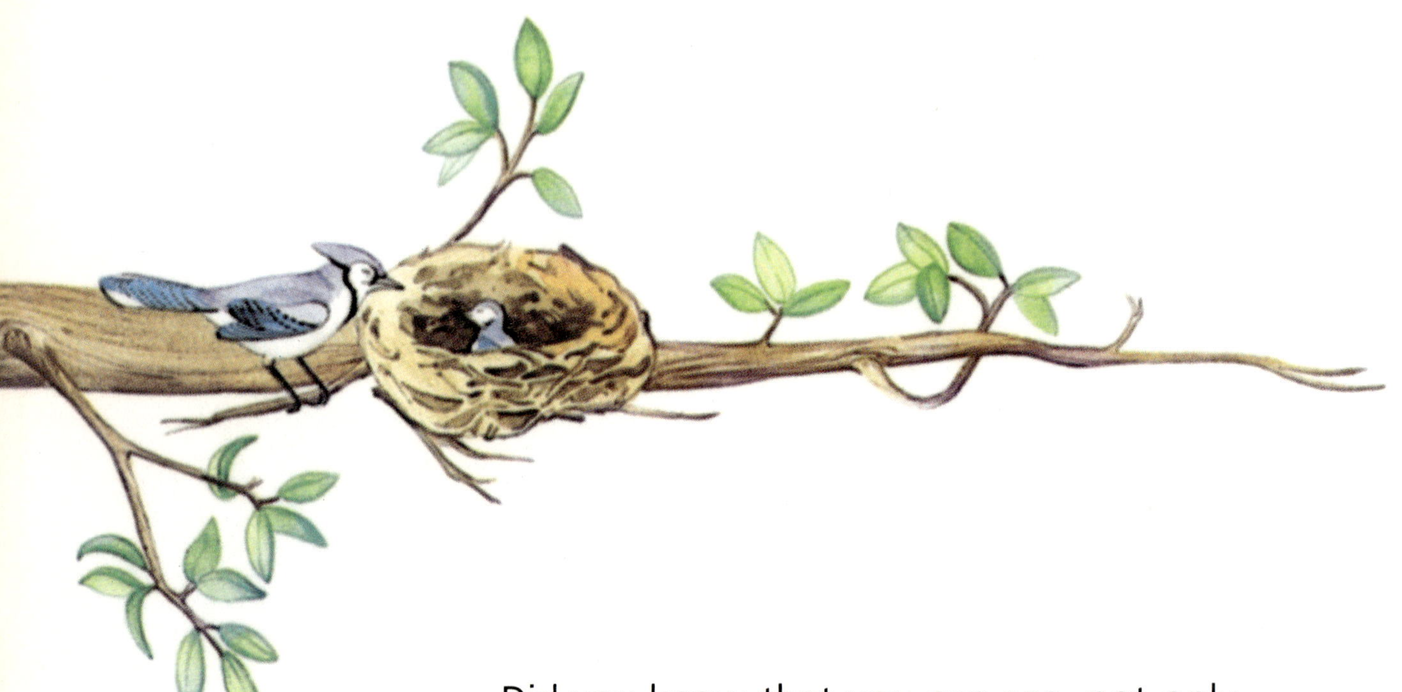

Did you know that you can see, not only with your eyes, but also with your ears, your nose, your mouth, and your touch? Your five senses help you learn about the world around you. They help you see, hear, smell, taste, and feel things.

Word pictures that tell how things look, sound, smell, taste, and feel are called **descriptions.** A description can make you see something even when it is not there.

Close your eyes and think about the word <u>tree</u>. What do you see? Is your tree tall or short? Does it have leaves or is it bare? Are its branches moving with the wind? Do you hear the wind? Do you hear birds singing in its branches?

Thinking Helps

1. When you look at something, try to look at it with all your senses. Try to see with your eyes, ears, nose, mouth, and hands.
2. When you describe something, use words that help your readers see, taste, hear, feel, or smell whatever you're describing.

Practice

A. Close your eyes and think about one word from this Word Box. Then write down what you see, hear, smell, taste, and feel when you think about the word.

circus	autumn	park	moon

____

____

B. Look outside your classroom window. Focus on one thing. List what you can see about that object with all your senses.

____

____

Using Exact Words ☑

Which sentence gives you a clearer picture
of the sky before sunrise?

> The sky was a pretty color.
> The sky was streaked with pearly pink.

The second sentence is clearer. The words
streaked with pearly pink are more **exact.**
They give you a picture of how the sky looked.

Use exact words when you write. Use the
Thesaurus on page 347 for help.

Prewriting Practice

Write each sentence. Use an exact word from
the box in place of each underlined word.

picked   sweet   hiked   purple

1. We <u>went</u> up a steep hill.

2. We <u>got</u> plums from a tree.

3. They tasted <u>good</u>.

4. They had <u>dark</u> skins.

Step 1: Prewriting—Choose a Topic

Maria listed all the things that she could describe. Maria thought about her list. Which idea would make the best description?

Aunt Ruthie

Maria had not seen her aunt for a long time. She did not remember her very well.

my secret hiding place

She decided to keep this a secret.

my hamster Puffy

Maria thought she could write a good description of her hamster. She certainly knew Puffy well enough! She circled the idea my hamster Puffy on her list.

On Your Own

1. **Think** Think about some people, places, or things you know well enough to describe. Use the Ideas page to help you. Make a list.

2. **Choose** Which idea would make the best description? Answer these questions about each one.

> Do I remember how this person, place, or thing looks? sounds? smells? feels? tastes? Would this idea interest someone else?

Circle a topic from your list. Then finish this sentence.

I want to write a description of ___________

3. **Try it** What will you describe? Do one of the activities under "Thinking About Your Topic" on the Ideas page.

Ideas for Getting Started

Choosing Your Topic

Topic Ideas

My desk   Today's weather   My bicycle

Description Starters

Do these pictures give you any ideas?

Thinking About Your Topic

Draw Some Details!

Think of something to describe. Draw it on a piece of paper. Show your picture to a classmate. Add more details if you need to.

Describing Words

Make a list of words that describe your topic. Think of words that tell how your topic looks, sounds, smells, tastes, and feels.

Step 2: Write a First Draft

Maria looked at the picture of her hamster. She thought of some words to describe Puffy. Then she wrote her first draft.

Maria's first draft

Puffy is ~~the~~ my hamstir. She feels nice. she's mostly brown. Puffy stuffs seeds into her cheeks, Her cheeks puff way out. Her water bottle wakes me up.

Think and Discuss ☑

- Which words tell how Puffy looks, feels, or sounds?
- What else would you like to know about Puffy?

On Your Own

1. **Ask yourself** Think about what you want to write. Answer this question.

   Which words would describe how my topic looks, feels, sounds, tastes, or smells?

2. **Write** Be sure your story has describing words. Do not worry about mistakes. You can make changes later.

Step 3: Revise

Maria read her description. She added more words to describe Puffy's paws.

Then Maria read her description to Doug. Doug liked hearing about Puffy, but he thought some things were not clear.

Reading and responding

Maria made more changes. Read her revised description on the next page.

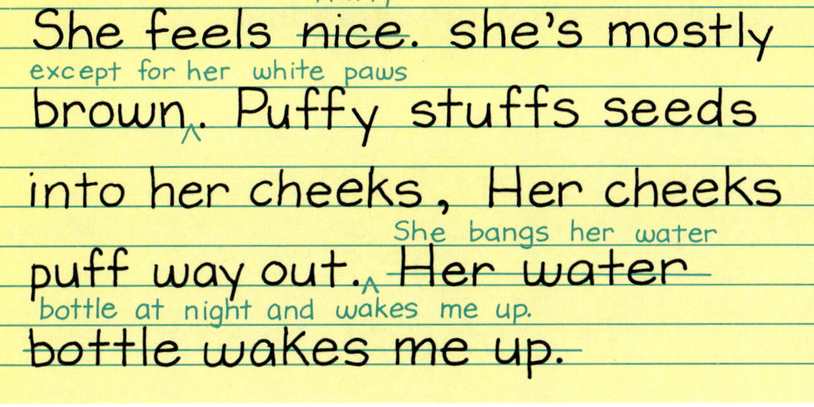

Think and Discuss ☑

- Which words did Maria add or change?
- Which sentence did she change? Why?

On Your Own

Revising checklist

☑ Where can I use exact words?
☑ What details can I add?

1. **Revise** Take out any words that are not clear. Add exact words. Add details.

2. **Have a conference** Read your description to a classmate. Make any changes that will make it better.

See the Thesaurus on page 347.

Step 4: Proofread

Maria was ready to proofread her paper.
She checked for mistakes and corrected them.

Maria's description after proofreading

> Puffy is ~~the~~ my hamstir. *(hamster)*
> She feels ~~nice.~~ *(fluffy)* she's mostly
> brown. *(except for her white paws)* Puffy stuffs seeds
> into her cheeks. Her cheeks
> puff way out. Her water *(She bangs her water)*
> bottle wakes me up. *(bottle at night and wakes me up.)*

Think and Discuss

- Where did Maria add a capital letter?
- Which end mark did she correct?
- Which word did she correct for spelling?

1. Proofreading Practice Each sentence has two mistakes. Write the sentences correctly.

a. My coat is redd

b. it has fiv snaps.

c. it is warm than my jacket.

2. Proofread Proofread your description. Use the checklist and proofreading marks.

Proofreading Checklist	Proofreading Marks
☑ **1.** Did I use capitals and end marks correctly?	∧ Add
☑ **2.** Did I use adjectives correctly?	— Take out
☑ **3.** Did I spell each word correctly?	≡ Make a capital letter
	/ Make a small letter

The Grammar/Spelling Connection

Grammar Helps
- Add <u>er</u> to compare two people or things.
- Add <u>est</u> to compare more than two.

Spelling Help
- The long **i** sound may be spelled i-consonant-e. (<u>five</u>, <u>kite</u>)

Step 5: Publish

Maria copied her description neatly. She checked it for mistakes. How did Maria make her description look special?

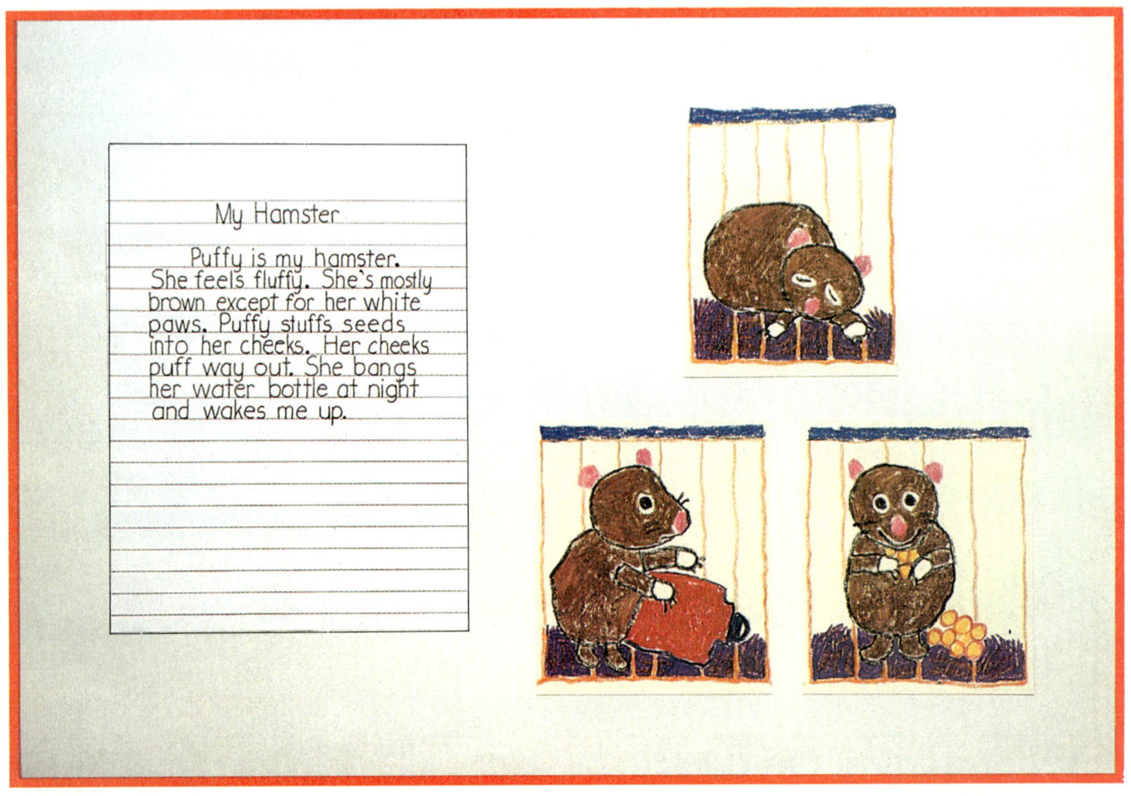

On Your Own

1. **Add a title** Write a title for your paper.

2. **Copy** Write neatly. Check for mistakes.

3. **Share** Show your description to someone.

Idea for Sharing

Match pictures and descriptions. First, all students should put pictures of their topics on the bulletin board. Then take turns reading the descriptions to the class. Who can find the picture that matches the description?

Applying Description

Writing Across the Curriculum
Music

When you listen to music, how do you feel? Can you describe the sounds? Here are some ideas for writing about music.

1. Enjoy the band. Pretend you are watching and listening to this marching band. What kind of music is it playing? Write a description of what you hear, see, and feel. You may want to use the words in the Word Bank.

Writing Steps

1. Choose a Topic
2. Write a First Draft
3. Revise
4. Proofread
5. Publish

Word Bank

drums
trumpets
flute
tuba
beat
rhythm

2. Listen to music. Your teacher will play some music. Listen carefully. Think of some words that tell how the music makes you feel or what it makes you think of. Use these words to write a description.

Nina enjoyed reading "The Day We Saw the Sun Come Up" by Alice E. Goudey. She liked to read stories about how things look and how people feel about them. Nina also read <u>The Little House</u> by Virginia Lee Burton. She made a picture report.

Think and Discuss

- What happens in the story?
- What exact words does Nina use?
- Why is this a good way to share a book?

Share Your Book

Make a Picture Report

1. Write the title and the author of your book on a piece of paper.

2. Draw pictures that show what happens in the story. Do not show the ending.

3. Write one or two sentences about each picture. Use exact words.

Other Activities

- Share your picture report. Show each picture in order. Remember to speak clearly.
- Paste your pictures on poster paper. Write the title and the author at the top.

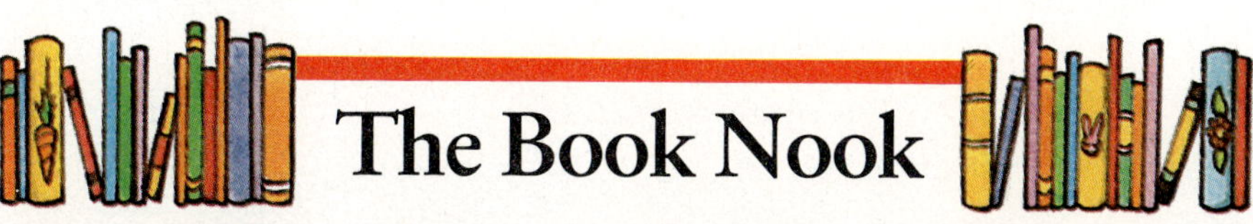

The Little Island by Golden MacDonald	**Where Can an Elephant Hide?** by David McPhail
An island changes with the seasons. Storms mean Kitten and other animals must be ready.	It is very hard to hide an elephant, even when the other animals help. What can Morris do?

Mechanics
Capitalization and Punctuation

January brings the snow,
Makes our feet and fingers glow.
February brings the rain,
Thaws the frozen lake again.

Sara Coleridge
from "The Months"

1 | Days

You know that there are seven days in a week. The names of the days of the week begin with capital letters.

Is the picnic on **Saturday**?

No, it is on **Sunday**.

Sunday	picnic
Monday	
Tuesday	
Wednesday	meeting
Thursday	
Friday	piano lesson
Saturday	

Guided Practice Tell which words need capital letters.

★ We went to the store on tuesday.
Tuesday

1. We baked bread on thursday.
2. On friday we cooked the eggs.
3. We made sandwiches on saturday.

Now write the names of the days of the week correctly.

1. _______________________________________

2. _______________________________________

3. _______________________________________

Summing up

▶ Use capital letters to begin the names of days of the week.

Independent Practice Write the answer to each question. Use the picture.

★ Which day is the party? Friday

1. Which day will the house be cleaned?

2. Which day is the class play?

3. Which day is the ball game?

4. Which day is Todd's birthday?

5. Which day is the picnic?

6. Which day is the club meeting?

Writing Application: A Story

Write a story titled ''A Strange Saturday.'' Why was the Saturday strange? What happened?

For Extra Practice, see p. 288.

2 | Holidays

Holidays are special days. Valentine's Day and Thanksgiving Day are holidays. Names of holidays begin with capital letters.

There are parades on **Labor Day**.

People play jokes on **April Fool's Day**.

Guided Practice Tell which words need capital letters.

★ We send cards on valentine's day.
Valentine's Day

1. When is lincoln's birthday?
2. School is closed on columbus day.
3. Did you remember mother's day?

Now write the names of the holidays. Use capital letters correctly.

1. _______________________________

2. _______________________________

3. _______________________________

Summing up

▶ Begin the names of holidays with capital letters.

★ June 14 is flag day.

June 14 is Flag Day.

1. This tie is a father's day gift.

2. Yesterday was memorial day.

3. April 1 is april fool's day.

4. January 1 is new year's day.

5. School starts after labor day.

6. Today is washington's birthday.

Writing Application: A Story
Write a story about a holiday you like. Why do
you like it? What do you do on that day?

For Extra Practice, see p. 289.

3 | Months

The names of the months begin with capital letters.

January	May	September
February	June	October
March	July	November
April	August	December

Guided Practice Tell which words need capital letters.

★ We planned the garden in march.
   March

1. We planted the seeds in may.
2. The plants began to grow in june.
3. Did the flowers bloom in july?
4. Most of them bloomed in august.

Now write the names of the months. Use capital letters correctly.

1. ______________________   3. ______________________

2. ______________________   4. ______________________

Summing up

Begin the names of the months with capital letters.

★ We camped in july.

We camped in July.

1. School started in september.

2. We got pumpkins in october.

3. In december we gave a play.

4. We wrote stories in february.

5. Spring vacation is in april.

Writing Application: A Description
Write a description of your favorite month.
What does the weather feel like? What do the
trees and flowers look like? What special foods
do you eat during that month?

For Extra Practice, see p. 290.

4 | Titles for People

Look at the pictures and names. Each name begins with a title. What are the titles?

A title begins with a capital letter. Which titles end with a period? Which title does not?

Guided Practice Tell how to write each title correctly.

★ mrs Jackson   Mrs. Jackson

1. dr Baker   **3.** miss Lane
2. ms Page   **4.** Mr Smith

Now write the titles and names correctly.

1. _________________________   3. _________________________

2. _________________________   4. _________________________

Summing up

▶ A title begins with a capital letter.
  Put a period after <u>Mrs.</u>, <u>Mr.</u>, <u>Ms.</u>, and <u>Dr.</u>
  The title <u>Miss</u> does not have a period.

Independent Practice

A. Write the titles and names correctly.

★ mr. Li 

1. Ms Hill _______________

2. dr Bok _______________

3. Mrs Hale _______________

4. miss Wu _______________

5. mr Hoy _______________

B. Write each sentence correctly.

★ My doctor is dr Perez.

My doctor is Dr. Perez.

6. His nurse is ms James.

7. They call me miss Cox.

8. My mother is mrs. cox.

Writing Application: A Story
Write a story about Mr. and Mrs. Mix-up.
Write about one of their mixed-up days.

For Extra Practice, see p. 291.

5 | Writing Book Titles

When you write about a book, you must write the title correctly. The first word, the last word, and each important word begin with a capital letter. The title is underlined.

The book **The Cat in the Hat** is funny.
I read **The Snowy Day** yesterday.

Guided Practice Tell how to make these book titles correct.

★ the seashore story   The Seashore Story

1. nate the great
2. george and martha
3. what mary jo shared

Now write the book titles correctly.

1. ______________________________

2. ______________________________

3. ______________________________

SOME BOOKS
WE HAVE READ

Swimmy
by Leo Lionni

Time of Wonder
by
Robert McCloskey

Mice Twice
by Joseph Low

The Happy Day
by Ruth Krauss

Summing up

Begin the first word, the last word, and each important word in a book title with a capital letter. Draw a line under the title.

Independent Practice Write these book titles. Use capital letters correctly. Draw a line under each title.

★ blueberries for sal

<u>Blueberries for Sal</u>

1. claude the dog

2. a letter to amy

3. the sunflower garden

4. owl at home

5. soup for the king

Writing Application: Creative Writing
Be an author! If you could write a book, what would it be about? Write a title for your book. Then write something that tells about the subject of your book.

For Extra Practice, see p. 292.

6 | Ending Sentences

A telling sentence tells something. A question asks something. What mark ends a telling sentence? What mark ends a question?

Tammy took a picture.
What does the picture show?

Guided Practice Tell the correct end marks.

★ The picture shows a turtle race.

1. Did they move very fast
2. Which turtle won the race
3. My turtle was second
4. The little turtle won

Now write the sentences correctly.

____

1. _______________________

2. _______________________

3. _______________________

4. _______________________

Summing up

▶ A telling sentence ends with a period.
▶ A question ends with a question mark.

★ We can see the city

We can see the city.

1. It is pretty at night

2. There are many lights

3. The lights are like stars

4. Where is our house

5. Can you see it

Writing Application: A Meeting
Whom would you like to meet? Write
questions you would ask that person. What
would you tell that person about yourself?
Write about yourself.

For Extra Practice, see p. 293.

7 | Commas in Dates

Every day has a name, such as Monday or Tuesday. Every day also has a date. A **date** tells a month, a day, and a year. A **comma ,** is used between the day and the year.

Penny was born June 21, 1978.

She started school on August 31, 1985.

Guided Practice Tell where to put a comma in each date. Then write the dates.

★ May 23 1987

May 23, 1987

1. January 5 1981
2. November 29 1988
3. March 8 1990

1. _______________________

2. _______________________

3. _______________________

Summing up

▶ A **date** tells a month, a day, and a year.
▶ Use a **comma ,** between the day and the year.

Independent Practice

A. Write the date in each sentence. Put a comma in the correct place.

★ Tim was born October 2 1981.

October 2, 1981

1. His brother was born March 5 1979.

2. His sister was born June 3 1985.

3. They got a puppy on May 12 1986.

B. Write a date to finish each sentence.

4. I was born __________________.

5. Tomorrow is __________________.

Writing Application: Creative Writing

It is fun to think about growing up. How old will you be in the year 2000? Write a story about what you would like to be doing on June 1, 2000.

For Extra Practice, see p. 294.

8 | Commas with Names of Places

Use a comma between the name of a city and the name of a state.

We watched fireworks in Tampa, Florida.

We went to a fair in Carmel, California.

Guided Practice Tell where to put commas.

★ Logan Utah   Logan, Utah

1. Lima Ohio
2. Topeka Kansas
3. Janesville Wisconsin
4. Helena Montana

Now write the cities and states correctly.

1. _______________________________

2. _______________________________

3. _______________________________

4. _______________________________

Summing up

▶ Use a comma between the name of a city and the name of a state.

Independent Practice Read each
sentence. Write the city and state named in
the sentence. Put commas in the correct places.

★ Nell is from Mesa Arizona.

Mesa, Arizona

1. I live in Clinton Iowa.

2. It gets cold in Nome Alaska.

3. Carlo moved to Salem Oregon.

4. Have you been to Flint Michigan?

5. My aunt lives in Duluth Minnesota.

Writing Application: A Description
Write a description of your town. Be sure
to use the name of your town and state.
Describe the special things you like about
your town.

For Extra Practice, see p. 295.

Grammar-Writing Connection

Writing Clear Sentences

all the children played they had fun

Did you understand the words above? Did you know that they are really two sentences?

All the children played. They had fun.

Good writers use capitals and end marks to help their writing make sense.

Revising Sentences

Write these sentences. Use capital letters and end marks.

★ see the snow it is winter

See the snow.

It is winter.

1. leaves appear spring has come
2. we have picnics we play

1. ______________________________

2. ______________________________

Grammar-Writing Connection

Creative Writing

The Lighthouse at Two Lights
by Edward Hopper
The Metropolitan Museum of Art
New York

Edward Hopper loved the ocean. This lighthouse is shown in bright sunlight.

• Does this seem like a lonely place? Why?

Activities

1. **Write about a visit.** Tell what you would see inside the lighthouse.
2. **Describe living in a lighthouse.** Tell what it would be like. Would you like it?

Check-up: Unit 10

Days (page 263)
Write the words that need capital letters.

1. My birthday is on monday.

2. The party will be on sunday.

3. It was on saturday last year.

Holidays (page 265)
Draw lines under the words that need capital letters.

4. Amy got a card on valentine's day.

5. We had a picnic on labor day.

Months (page 267)
Write the words that need capital letters.

6. Mark went to camp in july.

7. In march Meg got a puppy.

Titles for People (page 269)
Write each title and name correctly.

8. mr. Nye ___________________   **9.** mrs Pym ___________________

Writing Book Titles (page 271)
Write each book title correctly.

10. frog and toad together

11. the big mile race

Ending Sentences (page 273)
Write the correct end marks.

12. Where is Jason _____   **13.** He is in the park _____

Commas in Dates (page 275)
Write the dates. Use commas correctly.

14. March 2 1988

15. May 15 1989

Commas with Names of Places (page 277)
Write each city and state. Put commas in the
correct places.

16. Richmond Virginia

17. Chicago Illinois

Cumulative Review

The Sentence

Naming Part and Action Part (pages 39–44)

Write a naming part or an action part from the Word Box to finish each sentence.

1. _______________________ boiled.

| made soup |
| The water |

2. Mother _______________________.

Telling Sentences and Questions (pages 45–48)

Write the sentences correctly.

3. shall we go to the movies

____

4. a good show is playing

____

Nouns

Naming Words (pages 95–98)

Write the nouns.

5. The girl is cold. _______

6. The grass is wet. _______

One and More Than One (pages 99–104)
Write each noun to name more than one.

7. dress ____________________   **9.** spoon ____________________

8. man ____________________   **10.** box ____________________

Words for Nouns (pages 107–108)
Write the pronoun that can take the place of
the underlined word or words.

It	They
She	He

11. <u>Donna</u> got a bike. __________

12. <u>The bike</u> is red. __________

Verbs

Action Words (pages 151–152)
Draw a line under each verb.

13. Meg dances well.   **14.** She gives lessons.

Verbs That Tell About Now and About the Past (pages 153–156)
Draw a line under each correct verb.

15. Jody (draw, draws) a house.

16. Jody and Andy (paint, paints) it.

17. Yesterday they (paint, painted) a rainbow.

18. I (helped, help) them yesterday.

Name ___________________________

Cumulative Review, *continued*

Special Verbs (pages 157–166)
Draw a line under each correct verb.

19. Andrew's best friend (saw, seen) him.

20. They have (went, gone) to class.

21. Andrew's chair (is, are) new.

22. The old ones (was, were) broken.

Contractions (pages 167–168)
Write the contractions for these words.

23. do not _______________________

24. does not _______________________

Adjectives

How Something Looks, Tastes, Smells, Sounds, and Feels (pages 219–224)
Draw lines to make sentences.

25. The color is   loud.

26. The band sounds   cold.

27. The water feels   red.

28. The campfire smells   salty.

29. The soup tastes   smoky.

Adding er and est (pages 225–226)
Draw a line under each correct word.

30. This ball is (smaller, smallest) than that one.

31. This ball is the (smaller, smallest) one of all.

Capitalization/Punctuation

Days, Holidays, and Months
(pages 263–268)
Write the sentence correctly.

32. The first monday in september is labor day.

____

____

____

Titles for People, Writing Book Titles
(pages 269–272)
Write the titles correctly.

33. ms kent _________   **34.** dr snow _________

35. the bicycle man _____________________________

Commas in Dates and Names of Places
(pages 275–278)
Write commas in the correct places.

36. August 17 1987   **37.** Manhattan Kansas

Enrichment

Using Capitalization and Punctuation

Calendar Week

Make a calendar for next week like the one in the picture. Use one page for each day. On each day, write the month, the day, and the year. Use correct capital letters and commas.

On each day, write about something you did that day. Draw a picture of it.

Train Tracks

Write two short sentences about trains. Write a question and a telling sentence. Draw two train tracks across a sheet of paper. Draw and cut out cars for two trains. Make the cars big enough to have words written on them.

Write the words and end marks of the sentences on different cars. Paste the question along the top track. Paste the telling sentence along the bottom track.

1 | Days (page 263)

● ▲ Put a line under the words that need capital letters. Then write the words correctly.

★ On <u>tuesday</u> we gave a puppet show. 

1. School is closed on monday.

2. The spelling test is on wednesday.

3. Our class is having a party on friday.

■ Answer each question with a different day of the week.

★ When is the picnic? 

4. When is the baseball game?

5. When is your piano lesson?

6. When is the party?

2 | Holidays (page 265)

● ▲ Look at the pairs of sentences. Circle the one in which the holiday is written correctly.

★ We have a vacation on columbus day.

We have a vacation on Columbus Day.

1. I made dinner on Mother's Day.

I made dinner on mother's day.

2. We ate turkey on thanksgiving day.

We ate turkey on Thanksgiving Day.

■ Write the words that need capital letters.

★ When is flag day?   Flag Day

3. Friends visit on new year's day.

4. February 14 is valentine's day.

5. Did you forget father's day?

6. What day is labor day?

7. Is Monday veterans day?

3 | Months (page 267)

● ▲ Write the words that need capital letters.

★ Jason read four books in october.   

1. There was a big storm in january.

2. We had a class party in february.

3. In april it rained a lot.

■ Answer each question using a different month
of the year in a sentence.

★ When is it cold?

4. When do you go swimming?

5. When is your birthday?

6. When do leaves turn colors?

4 | Titles for People (page 269)

● ▲ Write the titles and names correctly.

★ dr pang 

1. miss white

2. mr sheehan

3. ms kemp

■ Find two names with titles in the story. Put a line under them and write them correctly.

The neighbors tried to make my baby sister Sally smile. First, <u>mr klein</u> wiggled his ears. Sally didn't smile. Next, mrs ito tickled Sally. Sally didn't smile. Funny dr rosas flapped his arms like a bird. Sally didn't smile. Finally, they went home. Sally smiled.

★ Mr. Klein

5 | Writing Book Titles (page 271)

● ▲ Write the book titles correctly. Draw a line under each one.

★ the garden 

1. oink and pearl

2. ben and me

3. sheep in a jeep

■ Write each sentence correctly.

★ I like **ira sleeps over**.

I like Ira Sleeps Over.

4. Who is **huge harold** about?

5. Jill read **jamaica's find**.

6. I love **james and the giant peach**.

6 | Ending Sentences (page 273)

● ▲ Write the correct end marks.

★ My uncle owns a farm __.__

1. He is happy there ____

2. Would you like to live on a farm ____

■ Write the sentences. Use correct end marks.

★ How old is Beth
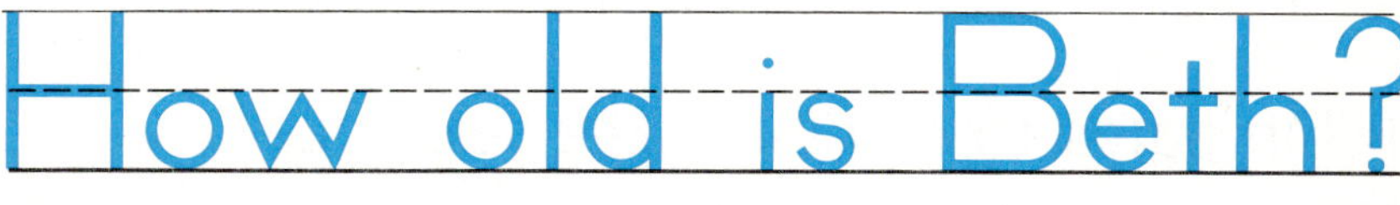

3. She is ten

4. Do you know her

5. I know Beth

6. Here she is

7. How are you

8. I am fine

7 | Commas in Dates (p. 275)

● ▲ Write each date. Use commas correctly.

★ July 4 1776

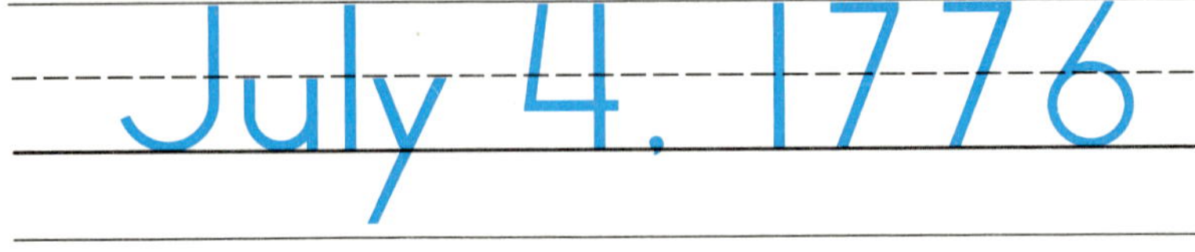

1. May 16 2001

2. June 12 1990

3. September 20 1970

■ Fill in dates to complete the sentences.
Write each date correctly.

★ School began  .

4. Today is ___________________________ .

5. School ends on ___________________________ .

6. Last Valentine's Day was ___________________________ .

7. Next New Year's Day is ___________________________ .

8 ‖ Commas in Names of Places (p. 277)

● ▲ Write each city and state. Put commas in the
correct places.

★ Canton Ohio 

1. Chico California

2. Dover Delaware

3. Townsend Texas

■ Write the city and state named in each
sentence. Put commas in the correct places.

★ My grandmother lives in Tacoma Washington.

4. Have you ever been to Portland Maine?

5. My family drove through Oxford Ohio.

6. Brownsville Texas is near the Mexican border.

Literature and Writing
Letters

Why is Sophie writing letters to her father?
What things does she tell him in her letters?

Dear Daddy

By Philippe Dupasquier

Dear Daddy,

I think about you lots and lots. Are you all right on your ship? We all miss you.

It's raining all the time at home, so Mommy bought me some red boots. They're great!

Mr. Green the gardener came to trim the hedge today.

Timmy's got a new tooth. He's got six altogether now. Mommy says he'll soon be walking.

I hope you are well. We think about you all the time.

Love,
Sophie

Dear Daddy,

School has started again. The garden is full of dead leaves.

The teacher showed me on a big map where you are going on your ship. She said it was a very long way. I wish you were home again.

Love,
Sophie

Dear Daddy,

When you come home, we'll do all sorts of things together. We can go walking in the woods, and fishing in the pond, just like we used to. At night-time we'll look up at the sky and you can tell me the story of the little prince who lives on a star.

It is not long till summer and I know we'll soon be all together again.

I think about you every day. Please come home quickly.

Love,
Sophie

Think and Discuss

1. Where is Sophie's father? What things does Sophie tell him in her letters?

2. Why do you think Sophie chose to tell her father about the things she did?

3. How is this story different from most stories you have read?

299

Rain

By Robert Louis Stevenson

The rain is raining all around,
It falls on field and tree,
It rains on the umbrellas here,
And on the ships at sea.

Think and Discuss

1. What does the poet mean by saying "It rains on the umbrellas here,/And on the ships at sea"?

2. Is rain important? Why do you think so?

3. This poem has **rhythm,** or a set of repeated beats. Listen as a classmate reads the poem. Tap out the beats in each line. Which lines have four beats? Which lines have three beats?

RESPONDING TO LITERATURE

The Reading and Writing Connection

Personal Response Think of someone you know. Write why you would miss that person if he or she went on a long trip.

Creative Writing How does the weather make you feel? Write a poem about weather.

Creative Activities

Answer Sophie's Letters Find a partner. Read aloud one of Sophie's letters. Have your partner pretend to be Sophie's father and answer the letter. Then have your partner read a letter and you answer it.

Take a Trip Pretend that you are on a ship. Where are you going? What do you see? Draw a picture and tell about your trip.

Vocabulary

A gardener is a person who gardens. What is a teacher? What is a firefighter? What other words end with <u>er</u> that name a person and a job?

VOCABULARY CONNECTION

Rhyming Words

Rhyming words end with the same sounds.

<u>Man</u> and <u>pan</u> are rhyming words.

Read the poem ''Rain'' again. Which words in the poem rhyme? Can you think of other words that end with the same sound as the poet's rhyming words?

Practice Write a word from the Word Box that rhymes with the word in dark print.

★ A **breeze** blew the ____trees.____.

sky	soon
blink	song
hand	trees

1. The **moon** will be out __________.

2. The sun shines **high** in the __________.

3. The **sand** is warm in my __________.

4. A singer sang a **long** __________.

5. Did I **wink** or __________?

302

Speaking: Making Introductions

Sophie's father was home. She wanted him to meet her friend Bob. She also wanted Bob to meet her father. Read Sophie's introduction.

SOPHIE: Daddy, I would like to introduce my friend Bob. He's in my class at school.

FATHER: How do you do, Bob.

SOPHIE: Bob, I would like you to meet my father. He is a sailor. He just returned from a long trip.

BOB: It's nice to meet you, sir.

When you introduce people, use these helps.

Speaking Helps

1. Always introduce a younger person to an older person.
2. Tell something about each person.

Practice

A. Introduce your teacher to someone in the class. Pretend that they have never met.

B. Choose two classmates. Pretend that the classmates have never met. Take turns introducing them to each other.

Thinking: Purpose and Audience

Sophie wrote letters to her father. Would her letters be different if she were writing to a friend? To her teacher?

If you were going swimming, would you wear your winter coat? We choose our clothes to fit what is happening. We choose our words the same way. We choose words to fit the person to whom we are writing or speaking.

Thinking Helps

1. Think about the person you are writing to.
2. Think about why you want to share something.
3. Think about what you want to say.
4. Think about the best language to use.

Practice

You have just moved and you want to write your best friend and your teacher.

1. List one thing you will tell your friend.

____

____

2. List one thing you will tell your teacher.

____

____

COMPOSITION SKILL

Kinds of Letters ☑

Some letters say thank you. Some letters tell someone to get well. Invitations ask someone to come to something.

What kinds of letters are these?

March 5, 1990

Dear Tom,

    I hope your leg is better. I am sending you a book about horses.

        Love,
        Aunt Gail

March 15, 1990

Dear Aunt Gail,

    Thank you for the super book. I love horses! I read the book all day.

        Love,
        Tom

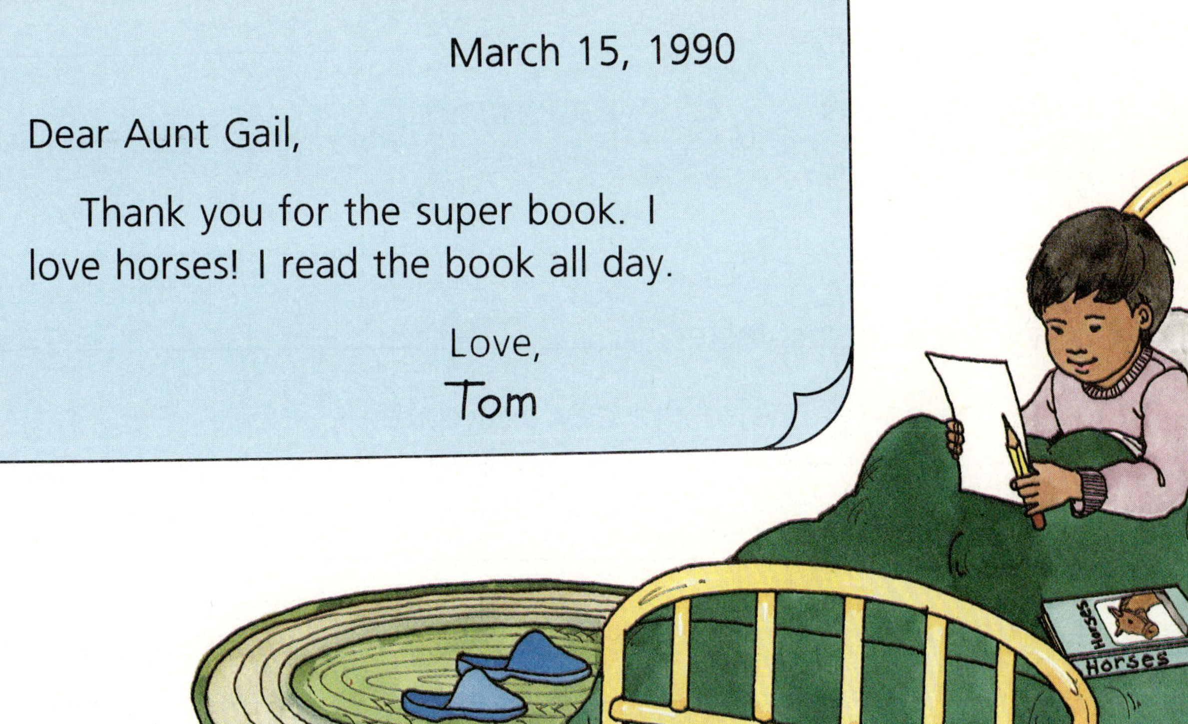

Prewriting Practice

Read the letter below.

July 13, 1990

Dear Tim,

Please come to my birthday party on Saturday, July 23. Come to Pine Lake at noon. We will go swimming.

Your friend,

Carlos

Now write the answers to these questions.

1. What kind of letter is this? Draw a line under your answer.

    a. thank-you letter   **c.** invitation

    b. get-well letter

2. Who will receive this letter? ___________________

3. When is the party? Write the day and date.

____

____

4. What time will it be? ___________________

5. Where will it be? ___________________

COMPOSITION SKILL

Parts of a Letter ☑

Sophie's friend Lori wrote Sophie this letter. A letter has five parts. What information did Lori write for each part?

date — April 29, 1990

greeting — Dear Sophie,

body — My new school is great. My class just did a TV show for kids. It will be on TV in June. Can you watch it?

closing — Yours truly,

name — Lori

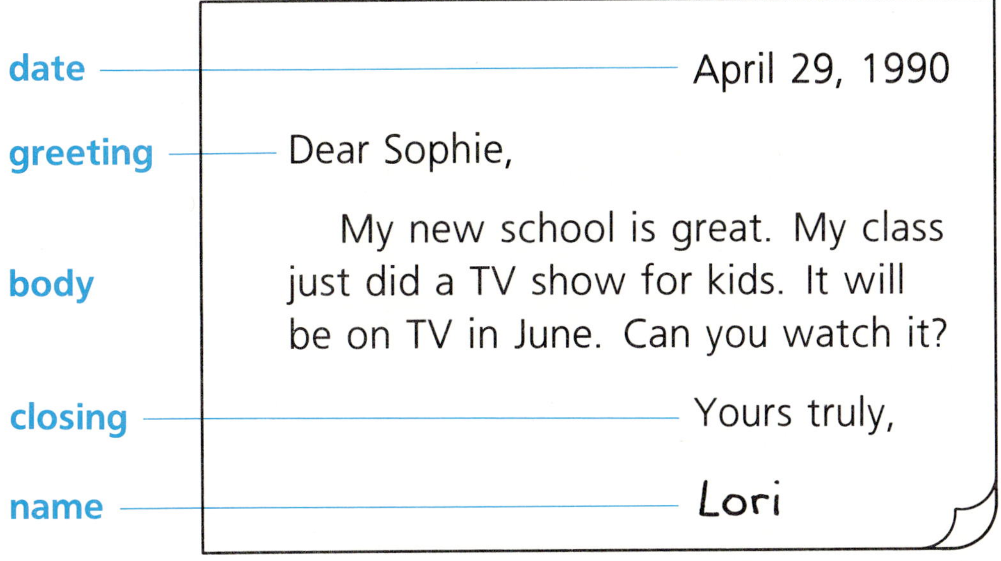

The **date** tells when the letter was written.
The **greeting** means ''hello.''
The **body** is the main part of the letter.
The **closing** means ''good-by.''
The **name** tells who wrote the letter.

- Which words in the greeting and closing begin with capital letters?
- Where are commas used?

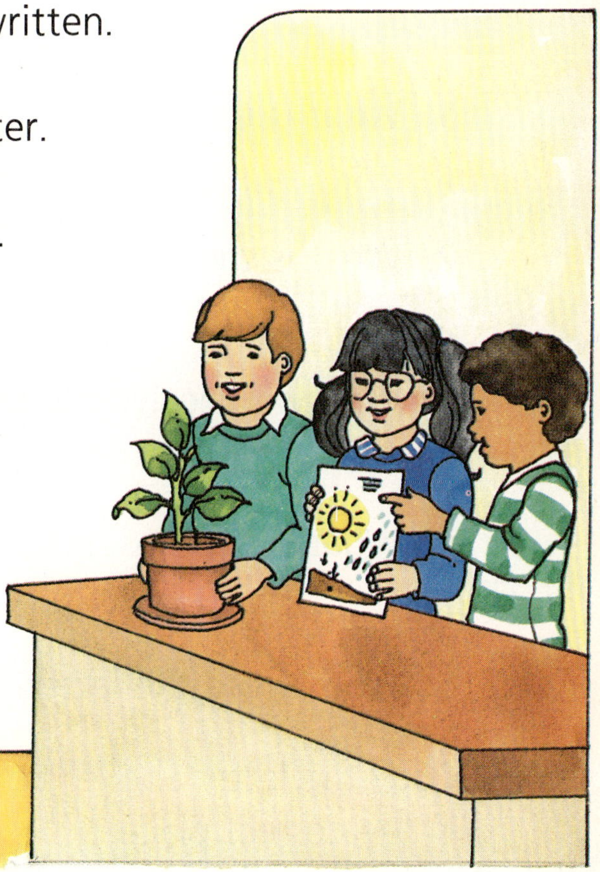

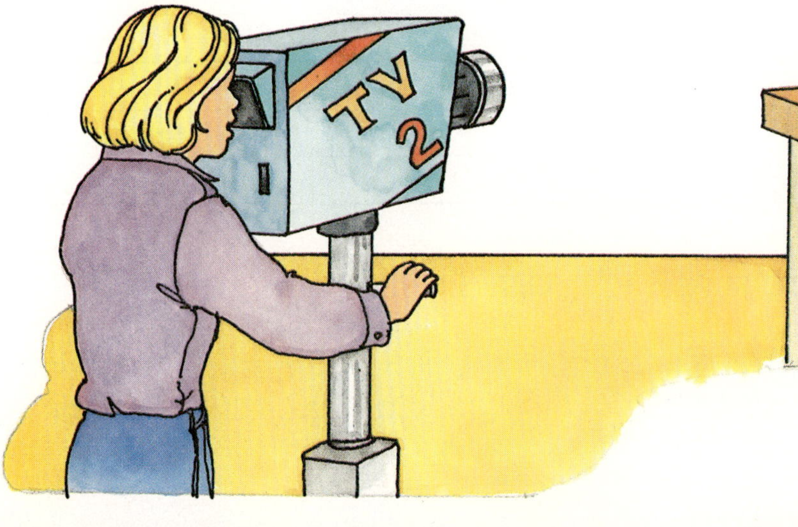

Prewriting Practice

Read this letter from Sophie to Lori.

> June 11, 1990
>
> Dear Lori,
>
> I saw you on TV. Mommy, Timmy, and I watched. We were so excited to see you! We really liked the show.
>
> Love,
>
> Sophie

A. Now write the answers to these questions.

1. What is the date? _______________________________

2. What is the greeting? _______________________________

3. Who will receive the letter? _______________________________

4. What is the closing? _______________________________

5. Who wrote the letter? _______________________________

B. Copy the letter above. Be sure each part is in the correct place.

The Writing Process
How to Write a Letter

Step 1: Prewriting—Choose a Topic

You can write a letter just to be friendly. Mike decided to write to Ms. Field. She had been his favorite babysitter. Then she moved to another town.

Mike thought about the things Ms. Field might like to know. He listed as many ideas as he could think of.

Mike wondered which idea to write about.

the ice-skating rink

It was big and exciting. Should he write about that?

the baby giraffe at the zoo

Mike knew that Ms. Field liked animals.

my cat's new toy

Ms. Field had always liked his cat. Mike knew she would love hearing about the toy. Mike drew a picture of his cat playing with the new toy.

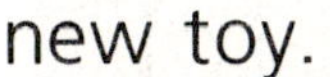

1. **Think** Think about who would like to get a letter from you. Write that person's name. Think about what you want to say. Use the ideas on the Ideas page to help you. List your ideas.

2. **Choose** Answer these questions about each idea.

   Do I want to write about this idea?
   Will this idea interest the person I am writing to?

   Choose an idea. Then finish this sentence.

   In my letter, I will write about ________________

3. **Try it** What will you write? Do one of the activities under "Thinking About Your Topic" on the Ideas page.

Ideas for Getting Started

Choosing Your Topic

Topic Ideas

A funny day   The surprise gift   My school

Letter Starters

Whom will you write to? Does this list give you
any ideas?

a new friend   your principal
a grandparent   a favorite cousin
a pen pal   a friendly neighbor

Thinking About Your Topic

Letter Strips

On strips of paper write as many ideas about
your topic as you can think of. Put your strips in
an envelope. Read your strips before you write.

Record It!

Talk into a tape recorder. Say all the things you
want to write. Listen to your tape. Does it
sound as if you are talking to the person you are
writing to?

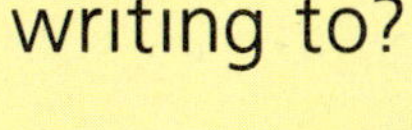

Step 2: Write a First Draft

Mike imagined talking to Ms. Field about his cat. Then he wrote his first draft. He did not worry about mistakes.

Mike's first draft

> May 5 1990
>
> dear Ms. Field,
>
> Do you rimember Hooper He has a new toy. I put it on the floor. He hits it and makes it move. Then he chases it and hits it ~~and~~ again. It is really funny to watch.
>
> your friend
> Mike

Think and Discuss ☑

• What else would you like to know about the cat and the toy?

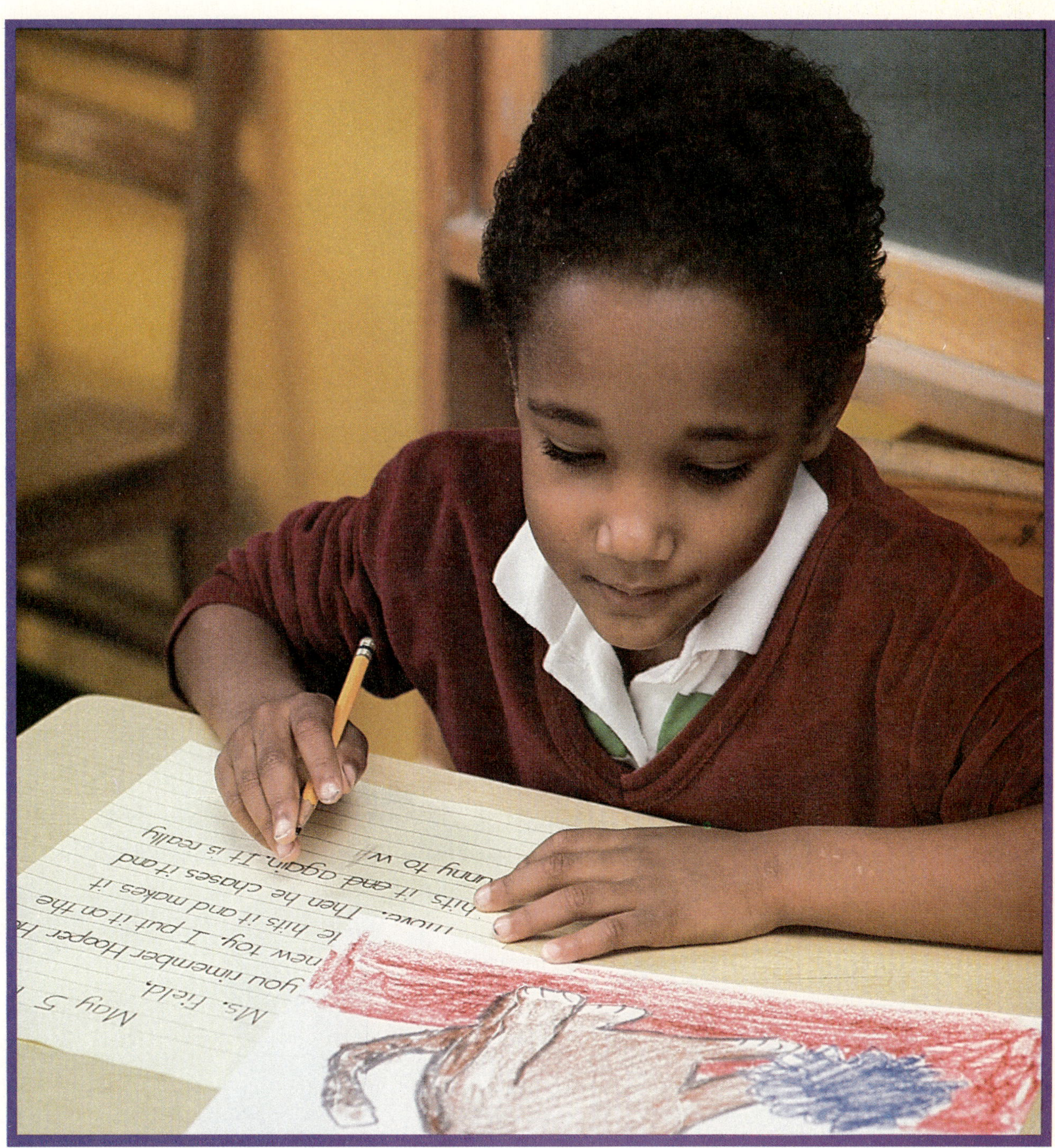

On Your Own

1. **Ask yourself** Think about what you want to say in your letter. What would the person you are writing to like to know?

2. **Write** Write your letter. Do not worry about mistakes. You can make changes later.

Step 3: Revise

Mike read his letter. He changed a word to make it clearer.

Then he read his letter to Justin. Mike asked Justin if he had any questions.

Reading and responding

Mike made more changes in his letter. Read Mike's revised letter on the next page.

> dear Ms. Field,
>   Do you rimember my cat Hooper He
> has a new toy. It is a pompom. I put it on
> the floor. He hits it and makes
> it move. jump Then he chases it and
> hits it ~~and~~ again. It is really
> funny to watch.

Think and Discuss ☑
- Why did Mike add a sentence?
- What other changes did he make?

On Your Own

Revising checklist
☑ What else could you add to make your letter clearer?

1. **Revise** Add words or sentences that will make your letter more interesting. Use clear details.

2. **Have a conference** Read your letter to a classmate. Make any changes that will make your letter better.

See the Thesaurus on page 347.

Mike was ready to proofread his letter. He checked for mistakes and corrected them.

Mike's letter after proofreading

> May 5, 1990
>
> dear Ms. Field,
>
> Do you ~~rimember~~ *remember* Hooper? He
> has a new toy. *It is a pompom.* I put it on
> the floor. He hits it and makes
> it ~~move~~ *jump*. Then he chases it and
> hits it ~~and~~ again. It is really
> funny to watch.
>
> your friend,
> Mike

Think and Discuss

- Where did Mike add commas?
- Where did he add an end mark?
- What other corrections did he make?

On Your Own

1. Proofreading Practice This letter has five mistakes. Write the letter correctly.

March 16, 1990

Dear Aunt Joan

   Did you have a happy birthday
I hope you liked the daysies?

love,

Ann Marie

2. Proofread Proofread your letter. Use the checklist and proofreading marks.

Proofreading Checklist
☑ **1.** Did I use capital letters correctly?
☑ **2.** Did I spell each word correctly?

Proofreading Marks
∧ Add
— Take out
≡ Make a capital letter
╱ Make a small letter

The Grammar/Spelling Connection

Grammar Help
- Use a comma between the day and the year.

Spelling Help
- The long **a** sound may be spelled <u>ay</u> or <u>ai</u>. (<u>stay</u>, <u>mail</u>)

Step 5: Publish

Mike copied his letter neatly. He checked it for mistakes. Then he addressed the envelope.

Mike's envelope

Mike's address

Ms. Field's address

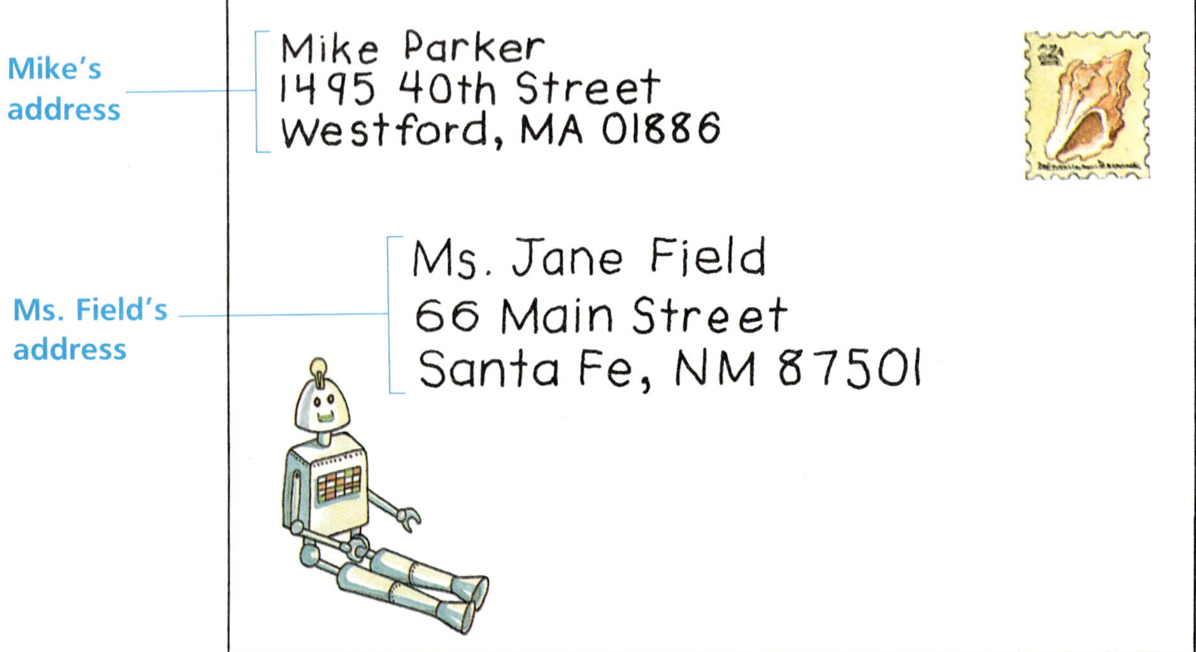

Think and Discuss

- Where did Mike put his address?
- Where did he put Ms. Field's address?

On Your Own

1. **Copy** Copy your letter neatly. Check for mistakes.

2. **Address** Put the person's name and address in the middle of the envelope. Put your name and address in the top left corner. Write clearly.

3. **Mail** Put a stamp on your envelope. Drop your letter in a mailbox.

Applying Letters

Writing Across the Curriculum
Health

One way to stay healthy is to exercise. Do you have a favorite sport or game? Do other people in your community like these activities too? You can find out by writing a friendly letter. Follow the five writing steps.

1. **Write to another class.** Write a letter to someone in another school. Write about your favorite game. Ask what game he or she likes best. Ask the person to write back. You may want to use the words in the Word Bank.

Writing Steps

1. Choose a Topic
2. Write a First Draft
3. Revise
4. Proofread
5. Publish

Word Bank

exercise
sport
gym
rules

2. **Write an invitation.** Do you know someone who knows a lot about exercise? Write an invitation to this person to speak to your class.

Mark liked the "Dear Daddy" letters. He wanted to read another story about a letter. He read <u>A Letter to Amy</u> by Ezra Jack Keats. He decided to share the book by making a big picture postcard. Here is his postcard.

Dear Jeff,
   This is a good book. Peter asks Amy to his party. He knocks her down when he runs to mail his letter. Now Amy is mad. Will she come to the party? Read the story.
      Your friend,
      Mark

Jeff Marcum
25 Lake Road
Athens, Ohio
     45701

Think and Discuss
- Who is the author of the book?
- Who are the main characters in the book?
- What did you find out about the story?

Share Your Book

Make a Picture Postcard

1. Get a piece of heavy paper. Cut it to the size you want your postcard to be.
2. Draw a picture for the story on one side. Write the title and author at the top.
3. Write a message on the other side. Tell about the book but do not tell the ending.
4. Write the name and address of a friend. Put the name, the address, and a stamp in the same places Mark put them.

Other Activities

- Read your postcard to your classmates.
- Display the postcard on the bulletin board.
- Mail your postcard to your friend.

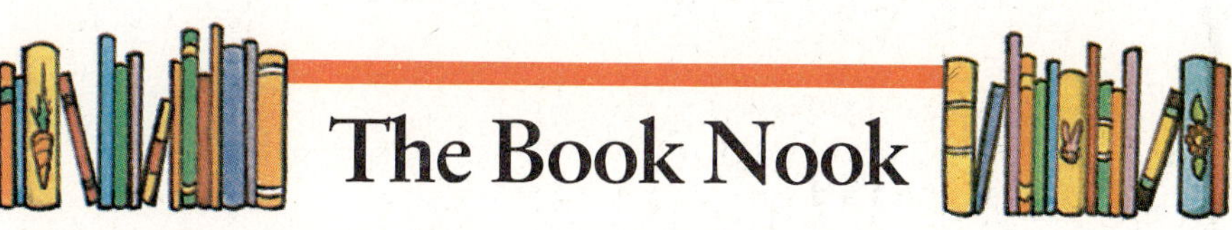

The Book Nook

Whistle for Willie	**Birthday for Frances**
By Ezra Jack Keats	By Russell Hoban
Peter cannot whistle. How can he call his dog Willie?	Frances is jealous of the plans for her sister's birthday.

Student's Handbook

STRATEGIES HANDBOOK

WRITER'S HANDBOOK

GLOSSARY

■ S T U D Y   S T R A T E G I E S ■

1 ABC Order

The letters of the alphabet are in ABC order.

**A B C D E F G H I J K L M
N O P Q R S T U V W X Y Z**

Words can also be put in ABC order. Are these words in ABC order?

ant   **b**ig   **c**at

The words are in ABC order. Use the first letter of each word to put words in ABC order.

Practice

A. Tell these words in ABC order.

dog	**i**nk	**g**ame	**e**at

Now write the words in ABC order.

1. _______________________________

2. _______________________________

3. _______________________________

4. _______________________________

B. (5–12) Write the missing letters.

A _____ C D E _____ G H _____ J K L _____

N O P _____ R S _____ U V _____ X _____ Z

C. Write the words in each box in ABC order.

13.
pet	_____
open	_____
nine	_____

15.
bear	_____
map	_____
hot	_____

14.
card	_____
with	_____
my	_____
sky	_____

16.
send	_____
glass	_____
hen	_____
zoo	_____

2 More ABC Order

You know that you look at the first letters of words to put them in ABC order.

Sometimes two words begin with the same letter. Then look at the second letter in each word. Why does <u>bat</u> come before <u>boy</u>?

bat   **bo**y   **bu**g

Practice

A. Tell these words in ABC order. Look at the second letter in each word.

s**e**ll	s**w**im	s**a**t	s**n**ow

Now write the words in ABC order.

1. _______________________   3. _______________________

2. _______________________   4. _______________________

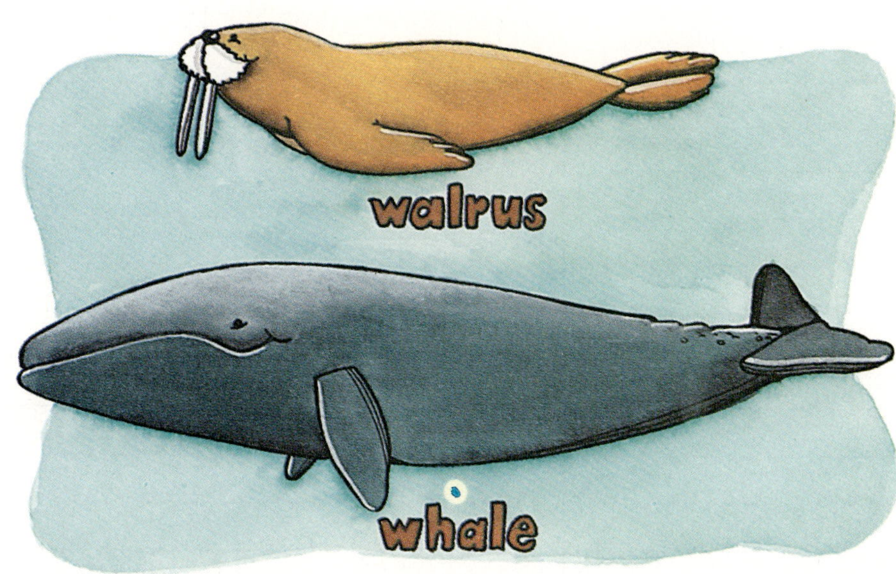

B. Write the words in each box in ABC order.
Look at the second letter of each word.

5.

blue ______________

ball ______________

bus ______________

8.

fox ______________

fly ______________

find ______________

6.

tan ______________

trip ______________

top ______________

9.

run ______________

ride ______________

rock ______________

7.

stand ______________

sing ______________

small ______________

10.

like ______________

let ______________

lunch ______________

Name _______________________________

3 The Dictionary

A **dictionary** is a book about words. The words a dictionary tells about are in **dark print.** They are called **entry words.** Entry words are in ABC order.

Entry Words

Practice

A. Answer each question with a word from the Word Box.

and	dig	girl	now

1. Which word is between <u>cap</u> and <u>fish</u>?
2. Which word is between <u>get</u> and <u>grew</u>?
3. Which word is between <u>mine</u> and <u>open</u>?
4. Which word is between <u>air</u> and <u>boy</u>?

Now write the words.

1. _______________________   3. _______________________

2. _______________________   4. _______________________

B. Write the word from the Word Box that comes between each pair of entry words.

box	need	arm	eat

5. baby _____________ cap   **6.** day _____________ fall

school	sun	some	swim

7. see _____________ stamp   **8.** sad _____________ seat

gym	give	grow	game

9. get _____________ glass   **10.** good _____________ gull

money	noise	quack	rock

11. pear _____________ ride   **12.** like _____________ nice

crow	carry	clam	cent

13. chop _____________ corn   **14.** copy _____________ cub

328 **Strategies Handbook**

4 Finding Word Meanings

A dictionary tells the meanings of words. Look at the dictionary entry for <u>mirror</u>. What is the meaning of <u>mirror</u>?

Entry Word   **Meaning**

Practice

A. Tell the meaning of <u>fog</u>.

Now write the meaning.

1. fog ____

B. Write the meaning of each word. Use the dictionary meanings shown on this page.

storm
A **storm** is a strong wind with rain or snow.

stripe
A **stripe** is a wide line.

subway
A **subway** is a train that travels underground through tunnels.

2. storm

3. stripe

4. subway

5 More Than One Meaning

One word can have more than one meaning. The dictionary explains each meaning. Each meaning is numbered.

How many dictionary meanings does the word <u>wing</u> have?

wing

1. A **wing** is a part of a bird, a bat, and some insects.

2. A **wing** is a part of a plane. It sticks out like the wing of a bird.

Practice

A. Tell which meaning of <u>wing</u> fits each sentence.

  1. The bird hurt its <u>wing</u>.
  2. I sat by a <u>wing</u> on the plane.
  3. A bee has two <u>wings</u>.
  4. I can see the silver <u>wings</u> of the plane.

Now write **1** or **2** to show which meaning fits each sentence.

1. _______   **3.** _______

2. _______   **4.** _______

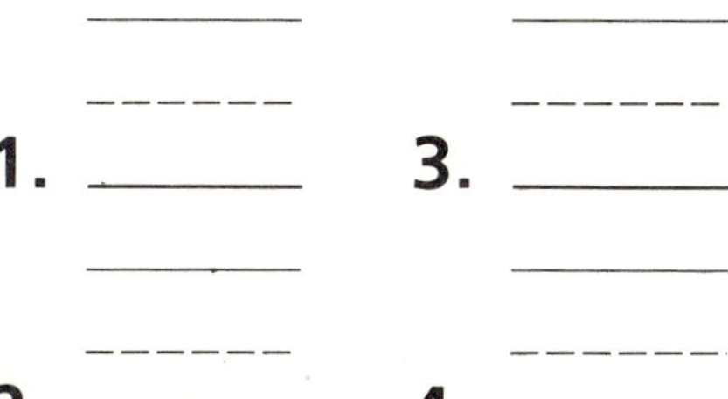

B. Write **1** or **2** to show which meaning of
<u>chest</u> fits each sentence.

chest
1. The **chest** is a part of the body. It is
below the shoulders and above the stomach.
2. A **chest** is a strong box.

5. Mother put the pictures in the chest. _______

6. Father is sunburned on his chest. _______

7. Ed has a pain in his chest. _______

C. Write **1** or **2** to show which meaning of
<u>spot</u> fits each sentence.

spot
1. A **spot** is a small mark that is not the
same color as the area around it.
2. A **spot** is a place.

8. Peter dropped the penny in this spot. _______

9. Lin got a black spot on her red dress. _______

10. The dog hid its bone in this spot. _______

6 Title Page and Table of Contents

The **title page** is the first important page in a book. It lists the book's title, author, and publisher.

The **table of contents** of a book shows the chapters, or parts, of a book. It shows the page where each chapter begins.

Practice

A. Find the title page on the first page of this book. Tell the title of this book.
Now write the title.

1. _______________________________

B. Look at the table of contents below. It has three chapters. Write the answers to these questions.

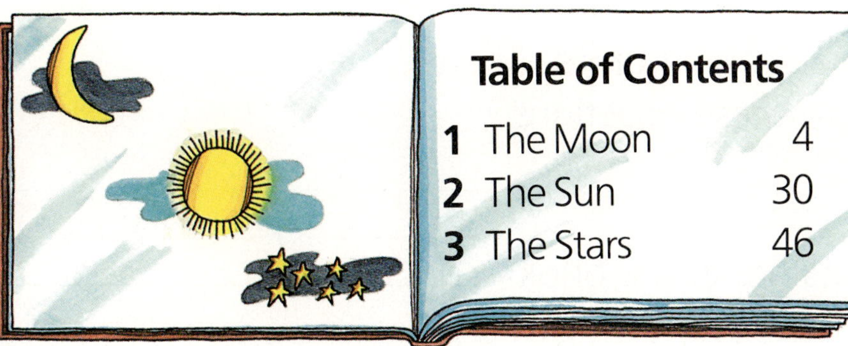

2. What is the title of Chapter 2? _______________________________

3. On which page does Chapter 1 begin? _______________________________

C. Write the answers to the questions below.
Use this table of contents.

> **Table of Contents**
>
> **1** Ants   3
> **2** Bees   15
> **3** Crickets   28

4. How many chapters are shown? _______________

5. What is the title of Chapter 1? _______________

6. What is the title of Chapter 3? _______________

7. On which page does Chapter 2 begin? _______________

D. Look at the table of contents on pages
3–8. The chapters are called **units.** Then
write the answers to these questions.

8. How many units are in the book? _______________

9. On which page does Unit 6 begin? _______________

10. In Unit 5, which story begins on page 125?

____

■ LISTENING, SPEAKING, THINKING ■

1 Listening for the Same Sound

Sometimes you hear the same beginning sound in different words.

Listen carefully as your teacher reads a poem. Which beginning sound is repeated?

You can hear the sound for <u>t</u> at the beginning of the words <u>tall</u>, <u>twinkly</u>, <u>tiny</u>, and <u>tail</u>.

What sound do you hear at the beginning of <u>can</u>, <u>carrot</u>, and <u>cress</u>?

Remember to use this help when you listen to a poem.

Listening Help

Listen for words that begin with the same sound.

Practice

Your teacher will read a poem to you. Listen for words that begin with the same sound.

2 Speaking to Give a Reason

When you want somebody to do something,
give a good <u>reason</u>. A reason tells <u>why</u>. A
good reason makes sense.

Imagine that your mother wants you to go to
bed early the night before your birthday party.

Your mother might say, "You should go to
bed early. Your birthday party is tomorrow. You
will be too tired to have fun if you stay up
late."

Your mother gave a reason why you should
go to bed early. What was it? Why was it a
good reason?

Practice

A. Think of something you would like to be able
to do. Finish this sentence.

I would like to _______________________________.

B. Why should you be able to do it? Give a good reason.

I would like to do this because _______________
____
____
____.

C. Tell a partner your reason. Then together think of another
reason.

3 How to Solve Problems

It was Mark's first day in a new school. He did not know anyone. What could Mark do?

Mark thought of three ideas.

1. He could keep his head down and wait for someone to say hello.
2. He could act silly to get attention.
3. He could say hello to some classmates, give his name, and tell something about himself.

Is each idea a good one? Why or why not? Which idea might Mark choose?

When you have a problem, use these helps.

Thinking Helps

1. Know what your problem is.
2. Think of more than one idea to solve your problem.
3. Try the idea you think is best. If it does not work, try another idea.

Practice

Suppose your baby brother or sister plays with and breaks your toys. List ideas to solve this problem. Explain why each idea might or might not work.

4 How to Classify

Some things go together because they are alike in some way. Which of these things are alike in some way?

The sun, the moon, and the stars are alike because they are things in the sky. What else is in the sky?

Practice

A. Draw a line through the word that does <u>not</u> belong in the group.

1. **People**	2. **Trees**	3. **Fruit**
teacher	pine	bread
firefighter	fish	apple
squirrel	oak	peach

B. Draw a line under the words that belong in each group.

4. **Vegetables**	5. **Animals**	6. **Colors**
milk	dog	red
beans	house	green
carrots	cat	yellow

5 How to Draw Conclusions

Read these sentences from "A Chair for My Mother." Rosa's mother saved coins in a big glass jar. Can you figure out why Rosa could not lift the jar? What clues does the author give you?

> Now the jar is too heavy for me to lift down. Uncle Sandy gave me a quarter. He had to boost me up so I could put it in.

The jar had a lot of coins in it. That is why Rosa could not lift it down. The words <u>too heavy</u> gave you a clue.

Authors do not always tell you everything. They want you to figure out some things. Words or sentences can give you clues. Things you already know can help you too.

Practice

Read these sentences. Write a sentence telling what Toni was doing.

Toni worked all morning! First, she put all her toys on the shelf. Then she made her bed and cleaned off her desk.

6 Cause and Effect

What happens when you fall off your bicycle? You probably cry. The first thing makes the second thing happen.

An **effect** is something that happens. A **cause** is what makes it happen. Falling off the bicycle is a cause. Crying is the effect.

Thinking Helps

1. When something happens, ask yourself what made it happen.

2. Ask yourself what might happen next.

Practice

A. What could happen if you touched a hot stove? Write a beginning for this sentence.

____

____________________________ because she touched the hot stove.

B. What could make a cat run away? Finish this sentence.

____

The cat ran away because ______________________

____

_______________________________.

7 How to Summarize

Read "Clouds" by Tomie de Paola on pages 240–241. Think about the most important ideas. Which idea below is not an important idea in "Clouds"?

1. Clouds are little drops of water or ice hanging in the upper atmosphere.

2. There are three main kinds of clouds.

3. Clouds look like puffs of cotton.

When you tell the important parts of a story, you are **summarizing** the story. Summarizing is a way to tell about the story in a short way, without telling the whole story.

Thinking Helps

1. First think about the most important parts of a story or book.
2. Summarize the story by telling the important parts.
3. Do not tell the whole story.

Practice

Read "Clouds" again. Write a short paragraph to summarize it. Tell the important parts. Do not tell every detail.

SPELLING GUIDE

Words Often Misspelled

A
again
already
any
are

B
been
believe
blue
both
bread
break
breakfast
brother
buy

C
come
could
country

D
dead
do
does
doesn't
done

door
dying

E
electric
eye

F
falling
feet
friend
from

G
give
glove
gone
great

H
half
have
head
helpful

I
I

K
key

L
laugh
let's
live
lose
love
lying

M
many
money

O
of

P
people
picnic
pink
pretty

R
roar
rolling

S
said
sew
some

T
teeth
they
think
to
toe
too
two

U
until

W
want
warm
was
wash
watch
what
who

Y
you
your

Spelling Guidelines

1. **A short vowel sound may be spelled a, e, i, o, or u.**

hat	bag
pet	ten
pin	mix
top	fox
fun	mud

2. **The long a sound may be spelled ai, ay, or a-consonant-e.**

mail	train
stay	may
game	plate

3. **The long e sound may be spelled e, ee, ea, or y.**

me	we
keep	green
read	clean
easy	happy

4. **The long i sound may be spelled y, igh, or i-consonant-e.**

fly	cry
high	light
nine	wise

5. **The long o sound may be spelled o or oa.**

go	old
boat	float
oak	load

6. The long **u** sound may be spelled <u>u</u>-consonant-<u>e</u>.

cute	use
mule	cube

7. The vowel sound in <u>cool</u> may be spelled <u>oo</u>.

food	room
boot	pool
noon	soon

8. The vowel + <u>r</u> sounds may be spelled <u>ar</u>, <u>or</u>, or <u>ore</u>.

art	car
form	born
more	shore

9. Two consonant sounds said close together may be spelled <u>br</u>, <u>cr</u>, <u>gl</u>, <u>sl</u>, <u>st</u>, <u>nd</u>, or <u>nt</u>.

brave	bread
crop	crack
glad	glass
slide	slip
step	fast
end	land
plant	hunt

10. The sound that begins <u>when</u> may be spelled <u>wh</u>.

which	wheel
why	while
what	white
whale	whisper

11. The consonant sound at the end of <u>stick</u> and <u>speak</u> may be spelled <u>ck</u> or <u>k</u>.

kick	rock
truck	quick
ask	milk

12. A final consonant sound may be spelled with the same two letters.

off	stuff
fell	shall
class	grass

13. The final <u>e</u> in some words is dropped before adding <u>ed</u> or <u>ing</u>.

saved	saving
loved	loving
used	using
traded	trading

14. The final consonant in some words is doubled before adding <u>ed</u> or <u>ing</u>.

hugged	hugging
stopped	stopping
planned	planning
grabbed	grabbing

15. Some words that sound the same do not have the same spelling or the same meaning.

see	sea
plane	plain
road	rode
tail	tale
hole	whole

Spelling Word Banks

Days

Sunday
Monday
Tuesday
Wednesday
Thursday
Friday
Saturday

Holidays

Columbus Day
Father's Day
Fourth of July
Independence Day
Labor Day
Memorial Day
Mother's Day
New Year's Day
Thanksgiving
Valentine's Day
Veterans Day

Months

January
February
March
April
May
June
July
August
September
October
November
December

Colors

black
blue
brown
gray
green
orange
pink
purple
red
white
yellow

Numbers

one	1
two	2
three	3
four	4
five	5
six	6
seven	7
eight	8
nine	9
ten	10
eleven	11
twelve	12
hundred	100

Shapes

circle
flat
line
point
round
square
straight
triangle

How to Use This Thesaurus

A thesaurus can help you find just the right words to use when you write. Imagine you wrote this sentence.

My birthday gift came in a **big** box.

You decide that **big** doesn't tell how big the box really was. You need to use a more exact word.

You can find other words for big in this thesaurus. The entry words in a thesaurus are in ABC order, so you turn to the B section and find big.

B

big having great size

That elephant is so **big!**
huge
large

You read the meaning of the word big. Then you read the sample sentence. You can see that large and huge are words you could use in place of big.

You decide that huge is the word you want. You rewrite your sentence.

My birthday gift came in a huge box.

My First Thesaurus

A

afraid filled with fear

The bird is **afraid** of the cat.
frightened
scared

argue to have a quarrel

They **argue** about the treat.
disagree
squabble

WORD BANK: Action Words

Use strong action words like these when you write.

climb	march	skip
crawl	ride	slide
dance	roll	walk

B

big having great size

That elephant is so **big!**
huge
large

brave facing danger or pain without fear

You are very **brave**, Mr. Bear.
bold
courageous
fearless

C

choose to pick out, after thinking about what is best

I will **choose** a dress to wear.
decide on
select

cold having no warmth

The wind is **cold** today.
chilly
freezing
frosty

cry to shed tears because of sadness or pain

Please don't **cry**, Little Bear.
sob
wail
weep

D

do to carry out an act

I will **do** my work now.
complete
finish

E

eat to take food into the body

They **eat** the corn.
consume
dine on
gobble up
munch

Use words like these to tell how things feel.

crunchy	hard	soft
crumbly	rough	sticky
dry	smooth	warm

F

find to get something by looking for it

Will she **find** the kitten?
discover
locate
spot

fun a good time

Playing soccer is **fun!**
enjoyable
entertaining

G

go to pass from one place to another

I will **go** as fast as I can.
advance
move on
progress

good having fine qualities

That is a **good** sand castle!
terrific
wonderful

350   Writer's Handbook

H

happy feeling pleasure

I was **happy** to see Uncle Ken.
delighted
glad

help to do what is needed or useful

I **help** Mrs. Wills.
aid
assist
lend a hand to

J

WORD BANK: Jobs

Use words like these to tell about people's jobs.

bus driver	firefighter
carpenter	nurse
chef	police officer
doctor	teacher

jump to spring into the air

Teeny and Tiny like to **jump!**
hop
leap

K

keep to put something in a safe or handy place

I **keep** my bones here.
save
store

L

laugh to make sounds to show that something is funny

Bear's costume made her **laugh**.
chuckle
giggle
howl

little small in size or amount

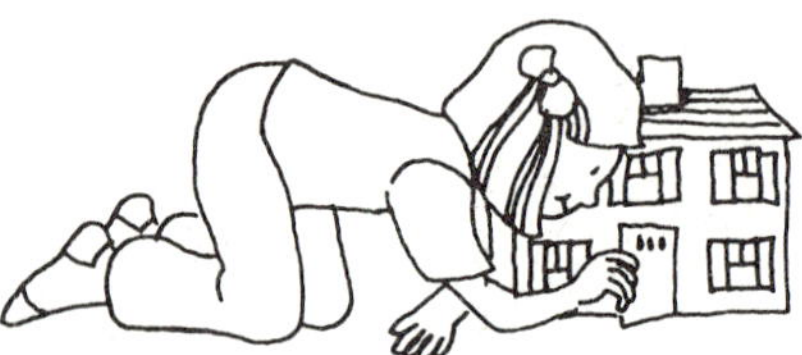

Abby has a **little** house.
miniature
tiny
wee

look to see

We **look** at a big lion.
gaze
peek
stare

M

mad feeling and showing anger

Why does Hen seem so **mad**?
angry
bitter
cross

make to form, shape, or put together

Ben and Tim **make** a fort.
build
construct
create

near close to

Our house is **near** the beach.
by
next to

nice kind and thoughtful

Fran is a **nice** person.
gentle
good
sweet

now at the present time

You must get on the bus **now**.
at once
immediately
right away

pat to tap gently with an open hand

I love to **pat** the puppy.
pet
stroke

WORD BANK: People

Use words like these to name people.

aunt	child	mother
boy	father	sister
brother	girl	uncle

WORD BANK: Places

Use words like these to name places.

city	ocean
country	park
house	school
lake	store
mountain	zoo

pretty pleasing to the eye

These are such **pretty** flowers.
beautiful
lovely

---

put to move something to a certain spot

Put the dishes on the table.
Lay
Place
Set

Q

quick very fast

Jill is **quick** at math.
speedy
swift

---

quiet with little or no noise

We were **quiet** in the library.
silent

R

rain to fall in drops of water from the clouds

It will **rain** soon.
> pour
> shower

ring a clear sound like that made by a bell

The loud **ring** woke up Ana.
> clang
> gong
> jingle

run to move quickly on foot

They will **run** around the track.
> dash
> race
> sprint

S

sad with no happiness or joy

Penny Pig is **sad** about her hat.
> gloomy
> unhappy

WORD BANK: Smell

Use these words to tell how something smells.

clean	fresh	stinky
fishy	salty	sweet
flowery	smoky	

said spoke aloud

Elli **said,** "I love my kitten."
declared
stated
exclaimed

---

shine to give off light

The stars **shine** in the sky.
glow
sparkle
twinkle

---

silly not serious

That is a very **silly** hat.
amusing
foolish
funny

---

smart having a quick mind

Paula is **smart** in science.
bright
clever
intelligent

WORD BANK: Sound

Use these words to tell how things sound.

barking	purring
cackling	quacking
clanging	soft
mooing	squeaky
noisy	whistling

stop to bring or come to a halt

When will the noise **stop**?
cease
end
finish

---

strange not usual

His coat is **strange**.
odd
unusual
weird

T

WORD BANK: Taste

Use these words to tell how something tastes.

bitter	spicy
fruity	sweet
salty	tart
sour	yummy

trip a passing from one place to another

They took a **trip** across the sea.
journey
voyage

---

try to make an effort to do something

Ana will **try** to win the race.
attempt
strive

U

under lower than

The mouse is **under** the lion's paw.
below
beneath

upset sad or worried

Dad was **upset** when we were late.
disturbed
nervous

W

wash to clean using water and soap

It's time to **wash** the dog.
bathe
scrub

wet being covered with a liquid

The **wet** bathing suits must hang to dry.
moist
soaked

Y

yell to call out in a loud voice

The people at the game **yell.**
scream
holler
shout

altogether   There are three children **altogether** in our family. I have 65 cents **altogether.**

apartment   An **apartment** is a place to live in a building. Some buildings have many **apartments.**

ash   **Ash** is left when something burns. It is soft and gray. The strong wind moved the **ashes** in the fireplace. **ashes**

atmosphere   The air that is around the earth is called the **atmosphere.** The **atmosphere** goes up for miles. Clouds float in the **atmosphere.**

banana   A **banana** is a fruit. It has a curved shape and a yellow skin. **Bananas** grow in warm places.

buy   I **buy** food with money. I **bought** our food at the supermarket. **Bought** is a form of **buy.**

catalog   We got a **catalog** in the mail. It is filled with pictures of toys, stuffed animals, and clothes. Father orders from the **catalog,** and the mail carrier will bring what Dad buys.

cauliflower   **Cauliflower** is a vegetable that has a head of small white flowers. **Cauliflower** is a healthful vegetable. It can be eaten cooked or raw.

charcoal   The black pieces that are left after wood burns are called **charcoal.** There was **charcoal** in the fireplace.

cirrus   High up in the sky are white and feathery clouds. They are called **cirrus** clouds. My favorite clouds are **cirrus** clouds.

comfortable   The soft chair is **comfortable** to sit on. My bed is **comfortable** to sleep in.

cumulus   Clouds with a flat bottom and a white fluffy top are called **cumulus** clouds.

curtain   A **curtain** is a piece of material that hangs inside a window. New **curtains** made the kitchen beautiful. **curtains**

deliver   The man will **deliver** a letter. The boy at the market **delivers** food.

dew   At night it is cool. Little drops of water form on the leaves and the grass. This is called **dew.**

earth   Plants grow in the **earth.** We live on the **earth.**

eastern   **Eastern** describes an area that is east. Sonia lives in the **eastern** part of our state.

elbow   The **elbow** is the middle part of the arm. The arm bends at the **elbow. Elbows** are hard.

empty   I **empty** the trash. Jan **empties** her coin jar. We **emptied** the boxes.

evening   **Evening** is a part of the day. **Evening** begins when the sun sets in the west.

exchange   To **exchange** something is to trade it for something else. Lisa and Rob **exchanged** books.

fasten   Mama will sew a button to **fasten** her skirt. We **fastened** our seatbelts. I am **fastening** my locket.

feathery   Something light and soft that looks like a feather is **feathery.**

field   A **field** is a large flat area of land. Horses ran in the **field.**

fig   A **fig** tree grows in warm places and produces brown and sweet fruit called **figs.**

fist   A **fist** is a hand that is closed up tight. I held the marbles in my **fist.**

fog   **Fog** is a cloud near the ground. It is hard to see through **fog. Fog** often gathers near the ocean.

frighten   To **frighten** is to scare. Loud noises do not **frighten** Alice. Zeno is not **frightened** of the dark.

furniture   Chairs, tables, beds, and desks are kinds of **furniture.** People work on, eat on, and sleep on **furniture.** It is made of wood, metal, or fabric.

grumpy   **Grumpy** means easily upset. You were tired and **grumpy** today.

heavily   The bowling ball fell. It dropped **heavily** to the floor. A big storm came. Rain fell **heavily** all day long.

imagine   Jane thinks about summer as the snow falls. She **imagines** herself warm. She **imagined** a dish of raspberries. What are you **imagining?**

jerk   The fish **jerked** the line. The old car looked funny **jerking** down the hill.

ketchup   **Ketchup** is a very thick, red liquid made from tomatoes and spices. **Ketchup** is put on foods.

laugh   A **laugh** is a happy sound that people make. My sister **laughs** at my jokes. We **laughed** at the movie. So much **laughing** made my stomach hurt.

leaves   **Leaves** mean more than one leaf. We helped rake the **leaves.**

machine   A **machine** is an invention that does work for people. A **machine** in our house that helps us is the dishwasher.

mare's tail   Mare is a word for a female horse. **Mares' tails** are feathery clouds that look like the tails of horses.

neighbor   Paul and Joe live next door to each other. Paul and Joe are **neighbors.**

nobody   **Nobody** means no person. **Nobody** can fly like a bird.

onion   An **onion** is a kind of vegetable. It can be red, green, white, or yellow, and has a strong smell. **Onions** grow underground.

outdoors   Jimmy goes out of his house to play. He goes **outdoors.**

pearl   A **pearl** is a smooth white gem. Something that looks like a **pearl** is called **pearly.**

potato   A **potato** is a vegetable with brown skin that grows underground. We had mashed **potatoes** for dinner. **potatoes**

puffy   Something that looks light and fluffy is called **puffy.** Clouds and smoke can be **puffy.**

pump   A **pump** is a low cut shoe. It slides on the foot. Mother wore a pair of **pumps. pumps**

quarter   A **quarter** is a kind of coin. Four **quarters** will buy the same things as one dollar. One **quarter** will buy the same things as 25 pennies.

sandal   A **sandal** is a kind of shoe with just a bottom and a strap. We wear **sandals** in summer. **sandals**

savings   **Savings** are money held aside. My brother took his **savings** and bought a bike.

scallop   A **scallop** is a kind of fish with a shell. The inside of the **scallop** is used for food.

September   **September** is the ninth month of the year. It has 30 days. **September** comes after August and before October.

shouldn't   I will try to be on time. I **shouldn't** be late. If it snows hard, there **shouldn't** be school. **Shouldn't** is a form of should not.

shovel   A **shovel** is a tool. It is made of a wide piece of metal joined to a long wooden handle. We dig holes with **shovels. shovels**

silverware   Forks, spoons, and knives that are made from metal are called **silverware.** Grandma used her best **silverware** at dinner.

soccer   **Soccer** is a sport. In **soccer** two teams run and kick a ball up and down a long field. Each team tries to score a goal.

sofa   A **sofa** is a long comfortable seat. We have a big **sofa.**

somebody   **Somebody** means some person. We do not know who won the race, but **somebody** must have won it.

spider   A **spider** is a very small animal with eight legs. **Spiders** make webs and catch insects in them.

stiff   I pitched the whole baseball game. Next day my arm was **stiff.**

storekeeper Somebody who runs a store is called a **storekeeper**. Bill paid the **storekeeper** for the milk.

stratus **Stratus** clouds are low, gray clouds. They usually bring rain or snow.

streak 1. The sun rising makes red lines in the clouds. Each line is called a **streak.** 2. The red color **streaks** through the clouds. The clouds are **streaked** with color too.

---

teaparty Zoe invites some friends over in the afternoon. They all sit at a table and drink tea in cups. Zoe is having a **teaparty.**

tomato A **tomato** is a round, red or green fruit. **Tomatoes** are used in salads. **tomatoes**

traveler A **traveler** is a person who **travels.** We met three **travelers** on the road. **travelers**

trim The barber will **trim** Jessica's hair by cutting some off.

tulip A **tulip** is a flower. It is shaped like a cup. **Tulips** come in many colors.

---

vegetable A **vegetable** is part of a plant that people eat. Carrots, broccoli, and peas are **vegetables. vegetables**

velvet **Velvet** is a soft, shiny material. Grandmother has **velvet** gloves. We saw a big **velvet** sofa.

---

waitress A **waitress** works in a restaurant. She brings people food and helps clean up. **waitresses**

web A **web** is a group of threads that a spider makes. Spiders make **webs** in special designs.

wrapper A **wrapper** is something that covers something else. Books can come in **wrappers.**

■ **I N D E X** ■

Numbers in **bold type** indicate pages where skills are taught.

Abbreviations, 269–270, 281, 286, 291

Adjectives
    forms of, **225–226,** 230, 235, 286
    identifying, **219–224,** 229–230, 231, 232–234, 285
    writing clearly with, 227

Affixes. *See* Suffixes

Agreement, subject-verb, 153–154, 163–166, 171, 172, 175, 176, 179, 180, 185, 284, 285

Alliteration, 335

Alphabetical order, 323–326, 327–328

Antonyms, 129, 130

Apostrophes, 167–168, 172, 176, 178, 187, **265–266,** 281, 285

Applying writing skills, 91, 147, 215, 259, 319

Art, writing about, 52, 112, 170, 228, 280

Audience, 15, 20, 85, 136, 250, **304,** 310, 311, 312–313, 319

Author, 13, 192

be, **163–166,** 172, 176, 185, 186, 285

Book report
    book jacket as, 216–217
    picture postcard as, 320–321
    picture report as, 260–261
    stick puppet as, 148–149
    writing a, **92–93**

Books
    parts of, **333–334**
    recommended, 93, 149, 217, 261, 321

Brainstorming, 14–15

Cadence, using, 300

Capitalization
    of book titles, **271–272,** 282, 286, 292
    of first word in sentence, **22, 45–46, 47–48,** 54, 55, 56, 61, 62, 88, 89, 143, 144, 145, 174, 211, 212, 213, 256, 257, 279, 316, 317
    of greetings and closings in letters, **307–308,** 317
    of proper nouns, **105–106,** 114, 115, 121, 174, **263–270,** 281, 286, 287, 288, 289, 290, 291
    writing clearly with, **279**

Cause and effect, 340

Characters
    analyzing, **70,** 128, 239, 299
    creating, 135–136

Charts, making, 71, 83, 137

Chronological order. *See* Sequence

Classifying, 83, **338**

Class story
    activities for writing, 16
    one idea in, 17
    the writing process and, 14–23

Clustering, 16

Colors, 346

Commas
    in letters, **307–308,** 317
    separating city and state, **277–278,** 282, 286, 295
    separating day and year, **275–276,** 282, 294

Comparison and contrast, 193, 241, 243, 299

Composition
    models, 305–308
    modes
        autobiographical, 71, 106. *See also* Personal narrative
    descriptive. *See* Descriptions
    expressive, 52, 71, 112, 129, 272, 280, 301, 309–319
    instructive. *See* Instructions
    narrative. *See* Stories
    skills
        exact words, using, **248**
        letter, parts of a, **307–308**
        letters, kinds of, **305–306**
        paragraph, what is a, **199–200**
        story, parts of a, **134**
        telling about one idea, **76–77**
        telling enough, **78–79**
        topic sentence, what is a, **201–202**
    steps in writing
        prewriting, **14–16,** 80–83, 135–137, 203–205, 249–251, 309–311
        writing a first draft, **17–18,** 84–85, 138–139, 206–207, 252–253, 312–313
        revising, **19–20,** 86–87, 140–142, 208–210, 254–255, 314–315
        proofreading, **21–22,** 88–89, 143–145, 211–213, 256–257, 316–317
        publishing, **23,** 90, 146, 214, 258, 318
    types of. *See* Class story; Descriptions; Letters; Personal narrative; Stories

Compound words, 72

Comprehension, literal, 13, 70, 128, 192, 239, 241, 242, 299, 300

Conclusions, drawing, 13, 70, 192, 241, 299, **339**

(Acknowledgments continued.)

Credits

Illustrations

Patience Brewster: 125–130 (borders), 125–128, 134 (top)
Lynne Cherry: 49, 131
Eileen Christelow: 165
Chris Czernota: 74, 75, 197, 199, 201, 202, 204, 205, 206, 211, 212, 216
Betsy Day: 32–35
Tomie de Paola: 240, 241
Philippe Dupasquier: 297–299
Laura Ferraro: 55, 56, 115, 177, 178, 231, 287
Charlie Hogg: 207, 208, 210, 214
Tim Jones: 76, 194, 246, 247
Mary Keefe: 21, 84, 87, 88, 138, 141, 143, 312, 315
Meg Kelleher Aubrey: 92, 93 (top), 147, 237–239, 242, 268, 318 (top), 320, 335
Susan Lexa: 25, 27, 31, 38, 41, 77, 78, 79, 91, 95, 96, 99, 101, 103, 105, 106, 108, 109, 110, 134 (bottom), 144, 151, 153, 155, 157, 162, 163, 164, 223, 224, 260, 265, 269, 273, 277
Jane McCreary: 164, 165, 217, 248, 271, 272
Stella Ormai: 189–194 (borders)
Linda Phinney: 65–72 (borders), 237–244 (borders)
Paul Michael Sances: 10–13 (borders), 93 (bottom), 251, 278, 321 (bottom), 337, 338
Millicent Selsam: 12–13
Gary L. Shellehamer: 297–301 (borders)
George Ulrich: 347–358
Lou Vaccaro: 37, 39, 43, 45, 47, 48, 57, 97, 107, 154, 156, 158, 159, 160, 161, 167, 219, 220, 221, 225, 263, 264, 266, 267, 275, 323–327, 329–334
Joe Veno: 26
Vera B. Williams: 65, 67

Hand marbleized French and English Cockerell paper from Andrews/Nelson/Whitehead Corporation, Long Island City, New York: 51, 111, 169, 227, 279

Photographs

1 Joseph Nettis/Stock Boston   **24, 188** Michal Heron   **28** Ken Lax   **36** Leonard Lee Rue III/Click/Chicago   **14, 15, 17, 18, 19, 20, 21, 23** Ken Lax   **40** Susan Van Etten/The Picture Cube   **64** Michal Heron   **71 M** Ken Stratton/The Stock Market   **71 L** Sam Sweezy   **71 R** NASA   **80 R** George M. Cassidy/Click/Chicago   **80 T** John Dommers/Photo Researchers Inc.   **80, 85, 86, 87, 88, 90** Ken Lax   **94** Dan McCoy/Rainbow   **124** Dave Schaefer/The Picture Cube   **135 T** Ken Lax   **135 B** Bobby Noel Kramer   **136, 138, 139, 140, 141, 142, 143, 145, 146** Ken Lax   **150** John E. Fogle/The Picture Cube   **218** Tom Algire Photography   **236** James H. Carmichael/The Image Bank   **249, 250, 252, 253, 254, 255, 258** Ken Lax   **259** Ellis Herwig/Stock Boston   **262** Dr. E. R. Degginger   **296** Michal Heron   **300 BL** Joseph Nettis/Stock Boston   **300 T** Mikki Ansin/The Picture Cube   **300 BR** Frank Siteman/The Picture Cube   **301 R** Russ Kinne/Photo Researchers Inc.   **301 M** Ed Gallucci/The Stock Market   **301 L** Walter Chandoha   **309 R** Ken Lax   **309 L** Vince Streano/The Stock Market   **309C, 310, 312, 313, 314, 315, 316** Ken Lax   **319** Norman Prince.

Fine Arts

52 *Doctor and Doll,* Norman Rockwell. Printed by permission of the Estate of Norman Rockwell, copyright © 1929, Estate of Norman Rockwell. **112** *Still Life with Three Puppies,* 1888. Paul Gauguin. Oil on wood, 36⅛ × 24⅝″. Collection, The Museum of Modern Art, New York. Mrs. Simon Guggenheim Fund.   **170** *Manchester Valley* (1914–18?). Joseph Pickett. Oil with sand on canvas, 45½ × 60⅝″. Collection, The Museum of Modern Art, New York. Gift of Abby Aldrich Rockefeller.   **228** *The Yearling,* Illustration by N. C. Wyeth from The Yearling by Marjorie Kinnan Rawlings. Illustration copyright 1940 Charles Scribner's Sons; copyright renewed © 1968 Charles Scribner's Sons. Reprinted with the permission of Charles Scribner's Sons.   **280** *Lighthouse at Two Lights,* Edward Hopper. The Metropolitan Museum of Art, Hugo Kastor Fund, 1962.

Cover Photographs

Cover and title page photograph: D. and J. Heaton/After Image

The photograph shows the Neuschwanstein Castle in Bavaria, a region in southern Germany.

Back Cover: Jon Chomitz